Green Learning Academy
www.greenlearning.com
(403) 873-1966
Calgary, Alberta

CHINA

Trudie BonBernard

ARNOLD
PUBLISHING LTD.

Copyright © 1998 Arnold Publishing Ltd.

ALL RIGHTS RESERVED

For more information or a catalog contact:
Arnold Publishing Ltd.
11016–127 Street NW
Edmonton, Alberta, Canada T5M 0T2
Phone (780) 454-7477
        1-800-563-2665
Fax (780) 454-7463
E-mail orderdesk@arnold.ca
        info@arnold.ca
Web site http://www.arnold.ca/

Author
Trudie BonBernard

Canadian Cataloguing in Publication Data
BonBernard, Trudie.
China

(Focus on global studies series)
Includes index.
ISBN 0–919913–88–1
1. China—Juvenile literature. I. Title. II. Series.
DS706.B66 1998   j951   C97–910630–3

Arnold Publishing Project Team
Project Coordinator: Judi McIntyre
Educational Editor: Phyllis A. Arnold
Editor: Betty Gibbs
Proofreader: Barbara Demers, Karen Iversen
Design: Linda Tremblay, Marcey Andrews
Production: Leslie Stewart, Linda Tremblay, Judy Bauer, Wayne Williams

Assisted by
Johnson Cartographics Inc., Wendy Johnson

Roth and Ramberg Photography

Illustrations/Maps
Louise Cheng, Mark Chez

Corel Corporation
Ottawa, Ontario, Canada

One image used herein was obtained from IMSI's *MasterClips Collection*, 1895 Francisco Blvd. East, San Rafael, CA 94901–5506, USA.

Mountain High Maps® Copyright ©1993 Digital Wisdom, Inc.
Tappahannock, Virginia, United States

©WorldSat International Inc., and Jim Knighton, 1997 Mississauga, Ontario, Canada. All Rights Reserved.

Manufacturers
Screaming Colour Inc., Friesen Printers

Cover Photos
Phyllis A. Arnold

Printed in Canada
Second Printing
11 500 copies in print

Photo Credits
Legend

AP	Arnold Publishing (Phyllis A. Arnold, Marcey Andrews, Judy Bauer)
GB	Glen BonBernard
CA	Canapress
CNTA	China National Tourism Administration
HKTA	Hong Kong Tourist Association
PS	Pat Somers
RF	Robert Fitzpatrick
NW	Nevada Wier
CH	ChinaStock
HD	Harbin Daily
CO	Corel Corporation

tl	top left	bc	bottom center
tc	top center	br	bottom right
tr	top right	b	bottom
ml	middle left	mt	margin top
mc	middle center	mm	margin middle
mr	middle right	mb	margin bottom
bl	bottom left		

Cover AP **iv** tl, ml GB **5**ml, mr AP; bl HKTA; tr GB; br CA **6** AP **8** 2, 3 GB; 1, 4, 5 AP **9** 6, 7, 8, 9, 11 AP; 10, mc GB **10**tl GB; 1, 3 AP; 2 CA **11**tr, ml NW; mr, b AP **12**ml GB; br AP **14** tl, 1, 2 AP; 3, 4 GB **15** 5, 6, 7, 9, AP; 8 GB **16** 10, 11, 12, 14 AP; 13 PS; bl GB **17** 15, 16, 17, 18, 19, mm mb AP; mt GB **18**tl, tr GB; mr AP **19** HKTA **21** AP **22** AP **23** AP **24** CA **25** AP **27** AP **28** AP **29** AP **32** GB **33** NW **34** 1 CNTA; 2, 3 NW **35**tl PS; tr CNTA **36** NW **37** NW **38** tl, mr NW; mc CO; br CNTA **39** NW **40** NW **41** NW **42** RF **43**tl RF; tr, mr NW **44**tr, tl, mr AP; br RF **45** 1, 2, 3 NW; 4 CH; 5 AP **47**tl CO; tr, bl, br AP **48** 1, 3, 4, 6 AP; 2 GB; 5 RF **49** 7, 12, 14 AP; 8, 9 GB; 10, 13 HKTA; 11 CO **52** HKTA **54** 1, 2, 3, 4 GB; 5, 6, 7 AP **55** 8, 9, 10, 12 AP; 11 GB **56** 1, bl AP; 2 GB **57** GB **58**ml, mr AP; tr GB **59**tl GB; mr, bl AP **60** GB **61** AP **62**bl, br AP; mr GB **63** AP **64**tl GB; br AP **65** 1, 2, 3, 4, 5, 8, AP; 6, 7, GB **66** AP **67**tl, bl, tr AP; ml GB **68** AP **69** AP **70** AP**71** AP **72**tl, bl, br AP; tr GB **73**tl, tr GB; mr, br, b AP **74** AP **75** AP **76** AP **77** AP **78**tr AP; mr GB **79**bl, br, tr AP; mr GB **80** AP **81** 1–9, mm AP; mr GB **86** 1,2,3,4,7 GB; 5, 6 AP **87** 8, 12 AP; 9, 10, 11, 13, 14 GB **88**tl GB; 1, 2, 3 AP **89** 4, 5, 7 AP; 6 GB **90** 8, 9, 11 AP; 10, 12 GB **91** 13, 14, mm GB; 16, 17, mt, mb AP **92** GB **94** tl, 1, 2, 3 GB; 4, 5 AP **95** GB **96**tl GB; 1, 2, 3, 4 AP **97** GB **98**tl, ml AP; bl GB **99**tl, ml, bl GB; b AP **100**tl, 2, 3 AP; 1, 4, 5 GB **101** 6, 7, 8, 10 GB; 9 AP **102** 11, 12, 14, 16 AP; 13, 15 GB **103**mr HKTA; br AP **104**tl, b AP; ml, mc, bl HKTA **105**mr, mt, mm, mb AP; br GB **107** AP **108**ml, mr, br AP; bl, tr GB **109** AP **112** AP **114** AP **115** AP **116** 1, 2, 3, 4, 6 HKTA; 5 AP; 7 GB **117** 8, 12 AP; 9, 11, 13 HKTA; 10 GB **118** GB **119** AP **120**tl, 4 HKTA; 1,2 AP; 3 GB **121** 5, 7, 8, mt, mm, mb HKTA; 6 AP **122** AP **123**tl, mr, br AP; tr GB **124** AP **125** GB **126** AP **127** AP **128**tl, ml, tr AP; bl, br GB **129** bl AP; tr HKTA **130** AP **131** 5, 8, mm, mb GB; 6, 7, 9, mt AP **132**tl, mr, br HKTA; ml, mc AP **133**tl, mr GB; tr CA; br HKTA **134** HKTA **135**tl, bl, tr, mr, mt HKTA; br HD **138** AP **139**bl, tr, mr, AP; b GB **140**tl, tr AP; ml HKTA; bl GB; mr CA

China Homepage
For information going beyond this textbook select the China homepage on the internet at http://www.arnold.ca/ and key in the five number code located in the inside front cover of your textbook.

ii

ACKNOWLEDGMENTS

I am indebted to Dr. Francis Yee of Camosun College in Victoria, Mr. Paul Clark of Shanghai, and Mr. Bob Fitzpatrick of Britannia Secondary School in Vancouver for their valuable advice.

While researching China's geography, I found information in *Geography of China* by Zhao Songqiao, *The Changing Geography of China* by Frank Leeming, and *Land of One Billion* by Christopher J. Smith extremely useful.

It was one of the joys of writing this text that I had the opportunity to work with the talented and creative staff at Arnold Publishing. Their efforts transformed this project through its many revisions from rough manuscript to finished product. I am especially indebted to Marcey Andrews for her book design and Linda Tremblay for her page design and layout. Their work makes the textbook inviting and student friendly. Special thanks go to Betty Gibbs for her skillful and greatly appreciated editing of the manuscript. She went through the text line by line suggesting improvements. Her thoughtful advice was always appreciated. Judi McIntyre coordinated all the details of getting this text to completion and kept us on task with good humor. Leslie Stewart and Judy Bauer deserve special thanks for their meticulous work with the many drafts and revisions. Thanks as well to Wendy Johnson who did the maps and to Mark Chez and Louise Cheng for the wonderful illustrations. Students who use this text will greatly appreciate these additions.

As always, thanks go to Phyllis Arnold. Her commitment to publishing materials that enrich student learning and stimulate thinking guided this project from beginning to end. Her input shaped every page of the text.

Finally, a grateful thank you to my supportive and patient husband, Glen BonBernard, who endured all the weekends and holidays I worked on this project. His encouragement, good humor, and continual support made this text possible.

Trudie BonBernard

Validators

Paul Clark
Canadian businessman
Shanghai, China

Robert Fitzpatrick
Social Studies Department Head
Britannia Secondary School
Vancouver, British Columbia

Dr. Adrian Leske
Professor
Religious Studies
Concordia University College of Alberta
Edmonton, Alberta

David J. Rees
Lecturer
Department of Modern Languages and
   Comparative Studies
Division of Slavic and East European Studies
University of Alberta
Edmonton, Alberta

Dr. Francis Yee
Instructor
Pacific Rim Studies and Geography
Camosun College
Victoria, British Columbia

We acknowledge the financial support of the Government of Canada through the Book Publishing Industry Development Program for our publishing activities.

Special Thanks

Alberta Intergovernmental and Aboriginal
  Affairs
Edmonton, Alberta

Bao Shing Chinese Herbal Ltd.
Edmonton, Alberta

Dr. Charles Muller
Professor
East Asian Philosophy and Religion
Toyo Gakuen University
Chiba, Japan

Ms. Ying Sun
Instructor
Pacific Rim Studies
Camosun College
Victoria, British Columbia

Dr. Francis Yee
Instructor
Pacific Rim Studies and Geography
Camosun College
Victoria, British Columbia

TO THE STUDENT

Canada and the United States have a long history of ties with China. In the past, thousands of Chinese immigrants came to North America to help build the railways and settle areas of the continent. Today, there are hundreds of thousands of North Americans of Chinese descent. Some of the largest Chinese communities outside Asia are found in North America. It is not surprising that many Chinese cultural events such as Chinese New Year are celebrated here. Chinese food is found throughout North America. Traditional Chinese herbal medicines, acupuncture, and *tai chi* are increasingly popular. Increasing trade with China is a goal of many North American businesses.

China's recent "opening to the world" policy now allows tourists and business people to visit China. Despite greater trade and cultural connections to China, we still know very little about life in this vast country. Foreign visitors often only see the large modern cities crowded with new high-rise office and apartment towers, shopping centers, and freeways. The heart of China lies outside the cities in the Chinese countryside. Over 800 million people live in small towns and villages in the countryside. While China has experienced enormous changes in the last few years, change happens much more slowly in the countryside.

On my own trips to China the journeys into the countryside are always the most exciting. They aren't always easy—China is an immense country with very rugged geography. It has some of the world's highest mountains, largest deserts and grasslands, and longest rivers. Travel to many areas of the country can be very difficult. Train trips stretch for several days. Roads are often unpaved. Sometimes the easiest way to travel is by boat along one of China's great rivers. No matter how difficult, though, going to the countryside is always worth the effort. Traveling in the countryside helped me understand the problems of making changes in this vast country. The difficulties of even providing food, housing, education, and jobs for a population of more than a billion people are enormous.

To help you experience the adventure of travel in China, I have organized this textbook around a North American student's trip through China. Taylor and her Aunt Heather travel to a few of China's largest cities, to the countryside, and to some of China's most remote regions. Their travels are based largely on my own travels. China is an incredible place to study and to visit. Enjoy your journey with Taylor!

Trudie BonBernard
January 1998

ABOUT THE TEXT

Organization of the Text

This textbook follows the travels of Taylor and her Aunt Heather through three regions of China. Each chapter in the textbook starts with Taylor's journal pages explaining what she and her Aunt Heather hope to research in that place. Journal pages usually appear as Taylor's printing on pages from her coil-bound journal. On page 58 you will see Taylor inputting her research notes and scanning her photographs into Aunt Heather's laptop computer. Pages 58–64 and 66–67 show her typed research on two Chinese villages.

Glossary

The glossary is provided to remind you of definitions of words that may be unfamiliar. Words printed in **bold** or on Taylor's definition notes on the journal pages are explained in the glossary on pages 148–151. Some words that are defined in the text are also included in the glossary to remind you of their meaning. If you find a word in the text that you do not understand, check the glossary for help.

Narratives

You will find short narratives throughout the text. They are identified by their light tan color and an open book symbol. Most narratives provide a Chinese person's view of life in China. The narratives are based on actual facts and events but portray the lives of fictional people. See page 13 for an example.

Points of View

"Talking Heads" are used to present various points of view on a given issue. While the characters are fictional the points of view are based on actual views expressed by Chinese people. See pages 76–77 for an example.

Titles

Titles in the text are coded by size and color in each section to help you make notes. It is easy to tell when a new idea is introduced by examining the size and color of the heading. Main ideas begin with dark red headings in capital letters. The title size gets smaller as ideas are explained in greater detail. (If you can read Chinese characters you will see that sometimes titles appear both in English and in written Chinese.)

Photographs and Illustrations

The photographs and illustrations have been carefully chosen to illustrate the concepts and issues presented in each chapter. Look at the visuals carefully and read the captions for more information.

Pronouncing Chinese Names

A brief guide to help you pronounce the names of the Chinese people and places in this book is found on page 79 in the section called Pinyin. On page 152 there is a pronunciation list of places Taylor visits and a few words of Mandarin she learns on her trip.

Tools of Learning

Learning How to Learn (SKIMM™) (found in the Appendix on pages 142–147) provides you with examples of a variety of strategies for collecting and organizing information, making comparisons, creating notes, recording vocabulary, and presenting your research findings. Refer to the ideas in the Appendix to help you complete the activities in the Looking Forward and Looking Back sections of the text. The icons are there to help you identify specific strategies you can use. Icons are explained on this page and pages 142–147.

China Homepage

Arnold Publishing invites you to visit our website at http://www.arnold.ca/ on the internet. For information going beyond this textbook, select the China homepage and key in the five number code located on the inside front cover of your textbook. This will take you into Learning How to Learn (SKIMM™) on Arnold Publishing's web page.

Check it out!

China Binder

Continuation of Taylor's Trip to China

Ongoing Project

CONTENTS

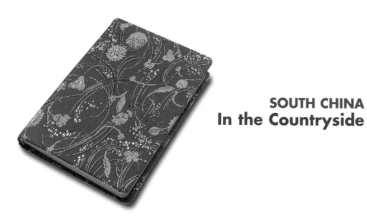

SETTING THE SCENE

Taylor and her Aunt Heather are packing for their trip to China. Aunt Heather is an international photographer and journalist. She is helping Taylor decide what to take on the trip. While on the trip Taylor will be doing research for a school project. She wonders how everything she needs will fit into her one small suitcase and backpack.

On the Way

I can hardly believe we are on our way to China. I thought Aunt Heather was teasing me when she asked me if I wanted to go with her on a trip through China.

When Aunt Heather was my age, she went to China with her parents. She kept a journal of her trip and gave it to me a few years ago. I've read it many times and I've wanted to see China for myself ever since.

One of the best things about this trip is that we aren't part of a tour group. We are going on our own. Aunt Heather is a photographer, writer, and an artist. She has been to China many times to take photographs for newspaper and magazine articles. Several years ago she spent a year in Beijing working for a North American newspaper. She speaks Chinese and has lots of friends in China.

Besides visiting Aunt Heather's friends we will also visit Xu Min's family in Shanghai. Xu Min is an exchange student who is living with Aunt Heather while she attends university.

Aunt Heather has several work assignments. She is to take photographs for articles on how countries in the Pacific Rim are becoming increasingly interdependent. She is also researching and writing a geography book on China.

My assignment is to keep a journal of my trip to China. My teacher expects me to make a presentation to the class when I get back.

The worst part of the trip so far has been the long flight. We've been flying for five hours and still have five more hours before we land in China!

At least the meals on the plane are interesting. I had to learn how to use chopsticks so I could eat the meal. A few noodles ended up in my lap, but by the end of the meal I could pick up even the smallest vegetable piece. We'll probably be using chopsticks and eating

Chinese meals most of the time on this trip so I need to practice. I wonder how I'll survive with no pizza or hamburgers!

Aunt Heather suggested I use these last few hours to organize my journal. I've decided my class would enjoy finding out how life in China compares with life where we live, and about how the Chinese people meet their basic needs. She says traditions and customs affect how people meet their needs. She suggested I could also research how technology is changing life in China. That sounds interesting, too.

I've brought maps, tour brochures, guide books, and some of Aunt Heather's old photographs with me so I can include information from these in my journal. I'm planning to take photographs of each part of the country we visit. China can be divided into three physical regions (North, West, South) based on elevation and climate. We will start in North China, fly to West China next, then spend the rest of our trip travelling in South China.

Aunt Heather is bringing her laptop and scanner to work on her assignments. I will be able to use them sometimes to type my own notes and scan some photos to include in the notes.

Aunt Heather also gave me a sketch pad just for the trip. I will be able to sketch what I see in China and include the drawings in my journal. She asked me to keep a list of any new words I don't understand so we can discuss them later. Making a China journal will be lots of work, but fun, too! I wish we were already there so I could get started!

旅途中

interdependent—needing each other
basic needs—basic human requirements that must be satisfied to avoid discomfort, pain, or even death; includes physical, psychological, and group needs
technology—the tools and skills of a group of people
traditions—ideas and ways of doing things passed on from older people to younger people for a long time
elevation—height above sea level
customs—the usual ways of doing things

LOOKING AHEAD

Cues to Learning

You will notice some words in **blue type** on this page and the Looking Back pages. These cuing words indicate the type of activity you are to do; e.g., **make**, **list**, **summarize**, **draw**, **present**. For suggestions, see the Appendix on pages 142–147 or the China homepage. (See page v for directions on accessing our homepage.)

Activities

1. Taylor and her Aunt Heather will be traveling by plane, bus, train, and river boat on their journey through China. Taylor wants to have only a small bag to carry. She has to be prepared for hot, rainy weather in the south, chilly nights in the grasslands, very hot weather in the deserts, and cold temperatures in the high mountains. Taylor also needs her notebook, guide books, sketching materials, camera, and dozens of rolls of film. That's a lot to pack into one small bag! Make a **list** of what you would likely take to China if you were going with Taylor and her Aunt Heather.

2. Taylor and Aunt Heather will need a passport for their trip to China. **Make** a passport for yourself or use the one provided by your teacher.

3. Taylor will keep track of her research findings in her China journal.

    Start a China binder for your research. A loose-leaf binder is easier for inserting pages. **Create** a title page for your trip to China and place it at the front of your binder.

    Prepare the following dividers and sections for your binder:
    a) a section for your notes, activities, maps, and illustrations called **Activities**, with chapter title pages for each chapter you study
    b) a section to record vocabulary called **WordBook**
    c) a section for your thoughts, ideas, and feelings on China called **China Journal**
    d) a section called **Tools of Learning** for information on how to learn and think.

4. Use one of the strategies for recording vocabulary shown on page 142 of the text to **record** the new vocabulary words Taylor identified on page 3. Put them in your China binder after the WordBook divider.

5. CHALLENGE. **Identify** which of the following symbols relate to China. You may have to do some research.

1
2
3
4
5
6
7
8
9
10
11
12
13
14

6.   Aunt Heather and Taylor each have a list of topics they want to research while in China. They would like your help in researching these topics and making a presentation on China at the end of their trip. You may wish to follow the research model on page 142.

 Topics for Research Projects

How do traditions and customs affect how the Chinese people meet their needs?

How do the Chinese people meet their needs and wants?

How does life in China compare with life where you live?

How is technology changing life in China?

How are the countries of the **Pacific Rim** becoming increasingly interdependent?

Pacific Rim—all the countries that border the Pacific Ocean. (See map in mini-atlas at back of book.)

Beijing, the Capital

I was so excited when our plane reached Beijing. Luckily I had a window seat and could take a few photographs of the city from the plane. What a huge city! It stretches for many kilometers in every direction.

After we collected our luggage and had our travel documents checked we took a taxi into the city. I expected China to look different from where I live, but the expressway into Beijing looks like the highways we have at home.

The new apartment buildings and office towers we passed also look just like the ones at home. Aunt Heather says that each time she comes to Beijing there are more new buildings.

The streets near the hotel are crowded with hundreds of bicycles. There are even special lanes for bicycles. I've never seen so many, and the riders ring their bells continuously! We walked along the sidewalk to the sound of tinkling bike bells. My class will be surprised to see pictures of all these bikes being ridden by adults.

There are lots of small shops in the neighborhood near our hotel. Stalls on the sidewalks sell food, furniture, books, and clothes. This is very different from home. Aunt Heather said neighborhood street markets are common in the cities.

We bought Chinese popsicles at a stall. They were shaped like wedges of watermelon with chocolate chips for seeds. They were terrific and very refreshing. Beijing is very hot.

The big surprise was the KFC restaurant a few blocks from the hotel. I thought there would be only Chinese food to eat here. Aunt Heather says we can eat at Pizza Hut tomorrow or even have a McDonald's hamburger.

My library books didn't mention hamburgers and pizza in China!

On our way back to the hotel we found a large group of people doing traditional dances under the expressway overpass. The sound of the drums was deafening! We had to cover our ears. One group wanted Aunt Heather and me to join them. They offered us fans and showed us how to twirl them. It looked like fun, but I was too shy to join in. On our way back to the hotel I bought my first souvenir, a bike bell for my mountain bike.

I'm very tired from the long flight, but almost too excited to sleep. Aunt Heather suggested I sketch a few things for my journal and plan what we will do in Beijing.

It will be a very busy week. Aunt Heather will be working on the geography of North China. She will print some pages for me to include in my journal. I want to visit the places where the Chinese emperors lived so I can find out more about China's history and the Great Wall. Aunt Heather will be visiting several government trade offices to take photographs and interview people for her article on China's part in the Pacific Rim. There's so much to do I can't wait for tomorrow!

天壇飯店
TIANTAN HOTEL BEIJING

住房卡
ROOM CARD

首都北京

travel documents—passport, visa
emperors—rulers of China
trade—the exchange of goods between countries
traditional—done the same way for a long time

What I want to find out in Beijing:
1. How does the geography of North China affect how people meet their needs?
2. How do people in China meet their transportation needs?
3. How do people in China meet their housing needs?
4. What historical buildings are found in Beijing? Why did the Chinese emperors build the Great Wall?
5. What is the system of government in China?
6. Why is trade with China important to Canada and the United States?

7

IMPRESSIONS

The trip to the hotel from the airport was incredible! I took an entire roll of film! I saw things I expected to see in a Chinese city, but I also saw things I never expected to see here. Beijing is an incredible mix of traditional Chinese features and modern features. No wonder Aunt Heather likes to come back here.

3. Bikes, bikes, bikes! Everywhere you look there are bikes.

1. The streets and sidewalks are crowded with people. More than I ever imagined!

2. Even when building modern high-rises traditional ways of working are used.

4. The buildings are a mixture of old and new.

5. Cellular phones are very popular. I saw more in Beijing than I do at home.

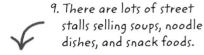

9. There are lots of street stalls selling soups, noodle dishes, and snack foods.

6. All along the way we saw lots and lots of people selling things on the street. This is the traditional way of shopping in China.

10. The skyline is incredible! So many big, new office towers. It makes you feel very small to stand on the street and look way up around you.

7. Some streets look a lot like home. There's a Pizza Hut and McDonald's near our hotel, and I saw a Hard Rock Cafe.

8. Whatever you want to buy, you can find it here in the big department stores.

11. Brand name running shoes are popular.

GEOGRAPHY OF NORTH CHINA

Landforms

- mountains and **plateaus** in west, hills and plains in east
- North China Plain and Northeast China Plain
- in 1556, worst earthquake ever recorded killed 830 thousand people in China
- in 1976, huge earthquake near Beijing killed over 250 thousand people

Rivers

- Huang He (Yellow River) flows across North China
- Huang He second largest river in China
- Heilong Jiang not widely used for transportation
- Heilong Jiang and Songhua Jiang freeze in winter

1 Winters in North China can be cold and snowy.

2 People need cool clothing for the hot, rainy summers in Beijing.

3 Boats are often poled along shallow sections of rivers.

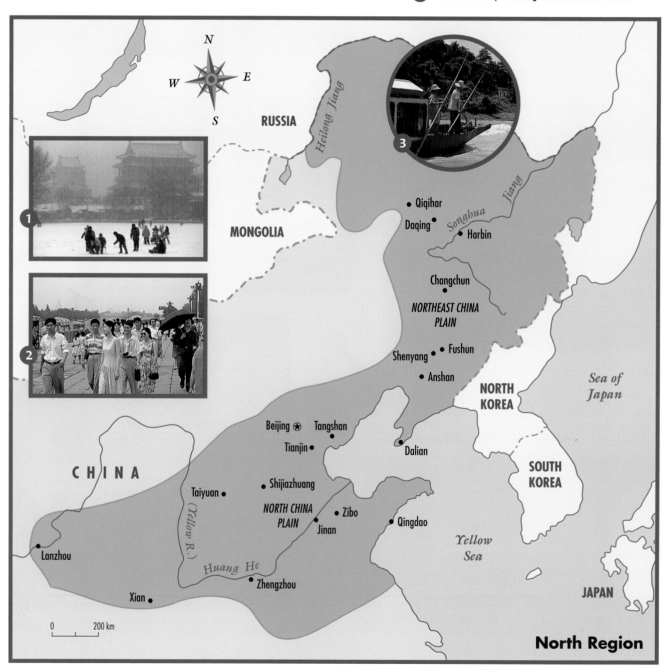

North Region

plateaus—landforms with steep sides and fairly level surfaces; often found between mountain ranges

Climate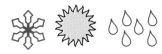

- long, cold, dry winters
- often snows in northern areas
- long, hot, humid summers
- moderate rain; 500–900 mm or less
- **drought** always a problem in interior areas
- most rain during summer
- frequent spring dust storms

drought—a long period of time without rain

Agriculture

- North China Plain and Northeast China Plain provide large areas for farming
- grow wheat, corn, **millet**, **sorghum**, cotton on North China Plain
- wheat, corn, sorghum, millet, sweet potatoes, peanuts, cotton, soybeans, sugar beets on Northeast China Plain
- too cold to grow vegetables in winter
- greenhouses increase vegetable crops
- cattle raised on grasslands in north
- pigs, chickens, reindeer, deer raised

19% of China's land area is in North China

35% of China's population lives in North China

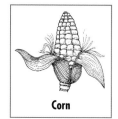

Wheat

Corn

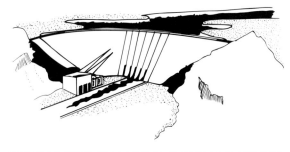

Soybean

Natural Resources

- large coal, oil, iron ore resources
- excellent land for agriculture
- rivers produce **hydroelectric** power
- gold, diamonds
- large timber resources
- fisheries

Transportation

- rivers too shallow to be used for transportation
- large network of railways in region
- railways mainly transport coal
- seaports very important for trade and **export** of coal and oil
- many new highways, expressways, and airports built recently

Population

- large population in North China
- 35% of China's population lives in North China
- 17 cities with populations over one million
- most people still live in countryside
- population almost all **Han**; small number of **minority nationalities**

BOTTOM RIGHT: Oil refinery and storage tanks in North China

millet—a cereal grain
sorghum—a tropical cereal grass
natural resources—raw materials that come from the environment, e.g., wood, water, fish, soil
hydroelectric—electricity produced by the force of water

export—goods sent to other countries
Han—the majority ethnic group in China
minority nationalities—ethnic groups other than Han, with their own language and culture

WINTER MORNING IN BEIJING

It was cold in the small apartment. Yi Ling snuggled farther down under the heavy blankets. He heard his mother and father as they hurried to dress for work. They would have breakfast at a **bean curd** stand near their factory. Grandmother took care of Yi Ling while his parents worked.

"Sleepy one, get up! It is after six o'clock," Grandmother called. She knew Yi Ling hated to leave his cozy bed so she waited until the last moment to call him. Reluctantly, Yi Ling slipped out of bed and changed from his wool pajamas into warm pants, shirt, sweater, and a padded jacket. They wore their padded jackets inside the apartment because even with the electric heater it was cold.

Yi Ling and his family lived in an older apartment block in Beijing. They had two rooms for sleeping and eating, a small kitchen, and a bathroom. Yi Ling wished their apartment had **central heating** like many of the new buildings. Last year Yi Ling's father applied for a new apartment, but it would be several years before they were assigned housing in a new building.

Yi Ling's grandmother turned on the water heater above the sink so he had hot water to wash. He ran water into a metal bowl and washed his face and hands. Then he started his chores.

As he swished his straw broom across the floor of the living room he looked around proudly. The gray cement walls were decorated with paintings and photographs of his family and relatives. The new color television and radio were on the dresser beside the new CD player. Yi Ling hoped to get a CD of his favorite singer next month. The two electric fans with their winter dust covers stood in another corner. They wouldn't be needed again until summer. Also crowded into the room were the refrigerator and a table and chairs where the family ate their meals. Grandmother slept in this room. Her narrow bed was pushed against one wall. Yi Ling shared the other sleeping room with his parents. Wooden storage chests were pushed under the bed and tall cupboards lined a wall. The apartment had no closets. Clothes and shoes were stored in wooden cupboards and storage boxes or hung on hooks along the wall.

After his chores, Yi Ling sat and chatted with his grandmother. This morning he ate a breakfast of soybean milk and wheat porridge. Some mornings his grandmother went to the nearby street market and brought Yi Ling fresh bean curd or golden deep-fried buns for breakfast. While he ate, Grandmother put on her padded boots, fur hat, and thick padded jacket with the red armband. Each morning she worked as a traffic helper, helping the crowds of pedestrians cross the busy street near their apartment.

His breakfast finished, Yi Ling called good-bye to Grandmother and grabbed his school books, mitts, scarf, and hat from the hooks by the door. He raced down the six flights of steps to the street. His friend Wu Shen was already waiting for him, clapping his hands together to keep warm. Many of Yi Ling's neighbors were using straw brooms to brush last night's light snowfall from the sidewalk and bicycle lanes of the street. People bicycling to work were bundled up in warm hats and jackets. Some had blankets thrown over their shoulders. Luckily, there were no freezing winds from the north today. Sometimes the north winds were so strong people had to push their bikes along the street. Today, only a slight breeze scattered the snowflakes drifting from the trees.

Wu Shen and Yi Ling were anxious to check the ice on the canal before going to school. If it was thick enough, they could ice skate after school. The two boys raced along the broad sidewalk toward the rivers. Their happy shouts echoed noisily along the frozen streets.

---

bean curd—tofu; a form of food made from soybeans
central heating—a furnace or boiler that provides heat to all the rooms of a building or apartment through pipes

GETTING AROUND

People in the cities meet their needs for transportation in a variety of ways.

1 It is a Chinese tradition to use human power as a way to transport goods and equipment. Hauling goods often provides jobs for people who have come to the cities from the countryside.

2 Bicycles are the most common form of transportation. There are over 11 million bicycles in Beijing, for example, and an estimated 250 million bicycles in China.

3 Bicycles are often used to carry parcels and goods around the city. It is not uncommon to see boxes of electric fans, air conditioners, televisions, or pieces of furniture tied to the backs of bicycles.

4 People sell fruit, vegetables, and other goods from bicycle carts at street markets. Morning street markets often start as early as 6:00 AM. Some **vendors** park their bike carts in front of busy bus or subway stations. People often shop on their way to and from work.

vendors—people who sell something

運輸

5 In the past bicycles were all black and of the same simple style. Today many types of bicycles are seen. Mountain bicycles have recently become available.

6 Many large cities have special lanes just for bicycles. There are often so many bicycles in these lanes that there are bicycle traffic jams!

7 Sometimes several hundred bicycles are seen lined up, waiting to get into a parking area on a city sidewalk.

8 Scooters and motorcycles have become very popular purchases. In the cities, shops often use these for deliveries.

9 The number of cars, trucks, and taxis in China has increased in the last ten years. Most are owned by the government or by companies. Individuals are now allowed to buy a car if they have enough money. Only very well-off people, however, earn enough to own a car.

10 Parking is a major problem in the city. Streets are narrow and not built for cars and trucks. Apartment buildings have limited parking spaces. Homes have no garages.

11 The increasing number of cars and trucks has created problems in the cities. Pollution from car and truck exhaust is a concern. Traffic jams are becoming a common feature of life in Beijing and other large cities in China.

12 In the past there were fewer than one thousand taxis in Beijing. Today, there are over 100 thousand taxis on the city's streets. Sometimes the taxis create their own traffic jams!

13 New freeways and highways have recently been built to serve all the new car, truck, and bus traffic. Road construction cannot keep up with the increasing number of vehicles in use.

14 Traffic lights are not common. Instead, a police officer stands on a yellow platform in the middle of the intersection controlling traffic with arm signals.

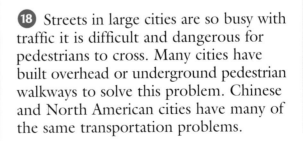

15 Like many large cities in China, Beijing has thousands of buses transporting workers, students, and shoppers around the city. Several cities are adding special bus lanes on main streets and adding hundreds of new buses to help transport more people. Buses are usually very crowded.

16 Many large buses are designed to bend in the middle so they can go around corners.

17 Several large cities are building subway systems to carry the millions of workers and shoppers through the cities.

18 Streets in large cities are so busy with traffic it is difficult and dangerous for pedestrians to cross. Many cities have built overhead or underground pedestrian walkways to solve this problem. Chinese and North American cities have many of the same transportation problems.

19 Minivans called "bread box taxis" are a new addition to transportation in Beijing and other large cities. Bread box taxis do not have a set route. People flag down a taxi and the taxi goes in the direction the group wants to travel.

LIVING IN THE CITY

The majority of workers in the city live in apartments rented from the government or their place of work. Some people still live in traditional **courtyard** homes. Many of these homes are being torn down and replaced by new high-rise apartments and **condominiums**.

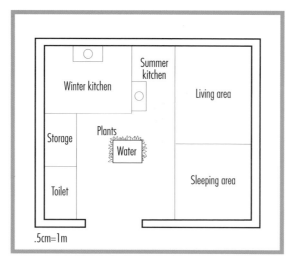

TOP LEFT: A traditional courtyard home.

BOTTOM LEFT: A kitchen, sleeping areas, and living areas are built around the paved courtyard of a traditional courtyard home.

Workers must apply to their **work unit** to be assigned an apartment. Often there is a wait of several years before an apartment is assigned. Company and government owned apartments are small, with only about four square meters per person. Rents are very low.

Owning a Home

Recently the government started to allow individuals to buy their own apartments.

Not everyone, however, can afford to buy a home. The cost of housing in cities like Beijing is very high. Only a small percentage of city residents own their own homes. Some families who have started their own businesses and become wealthy are able to buy luxurious new apartments in high-rise buildings. Only the very wealthy can afford to live in luxury condominiums and private homes. For millions of people in the cities owning a home is still a dream.

courtyard—an open space surrounded by walls or buildings
condominiums—two or more homes or apartments that are joined together but have separate owners
work unit—a Chinese term referring to the place where people work

THE NEW APARTMENT

Wang Zi wheeled into the bicycle lane and slowly merged with the flood of bicycles heading toward the city. The other riders were in a hurry to get to work. Many noisily jingled their bicycle bells. Wang Zi was in no hurry. He was retired.

Every day since the family had moved to the new apartment, Wang Zi rode back to his old neighborhood. His family kept telling him that he would learn to like the new apartment as much as they did. Wang Zi wondered. The day the bicycle moving-vans had moved their beds, furniture, television, refrigerator, and washing machine had been one of his saddest days.

Wang Zi, his youngest daughter, son, daughter-in-law, and grandson shared the new apartment. The family was thrilled that they now had four rooms, central heating, a gas stove, an electric water heater, and their own shower and toilet. They no longer had to share a bathroom with the two other families that had been crowded into the small courtyard home.

Wang Zi agreed with his family that the new apartment was more comfortable. Still, he missed his old home. He missed the morning walk to the park with his cage of songbirds. He had often sat in the park with other bird owners and listened to their birds teach each other songs. He missed the activity of the vendors in the lanes and the nearby shops. In the new apartment, he felt trapped on the third floor.

He didn't know his neighbors. There was no park, no shops, or market nearby. Wang Zi's grandson loved the larger apartment. He didn't miss the old neighborhood. Wang Zi's son and daughter were too busy with their jobs to miss their old neighborhood. And, as they constantly reminded him, they had had no choice about moving.

A year ago, the city government sent them a notice telling them their courtyard home required too many repairs. The land was sold to a company to build a new high-rise block of luxury apartments.

The new apartments were too expensive for Wang Zi's family. Instead, they moved to an apartment block owned by the company where his son worked. Wang Zi's son had waited three years to be assigned an apartment. The rent was ten times what the family had paid for the city-owned courtyard home. That worried Wang Zi, but his children were confident about the future. Both had started small businesses in addition to their company jobs. They talked of the family one day buying their own apartment.

As he neared his old neighborhood, Wang Zi felt his heart warm in recognition. This was where he had expected to spend his retirement years. Now, each week another building disappeared. Construction crews worked on the apartment block and a new overpass for the freeway nearby. Soon there would be little left of the old neighborhood. Wang Zi worried about how he would spend his days when everything was gone. But today, as he wheeled his bicycle into a former neighbor's courtyard, he felt that he had come home.

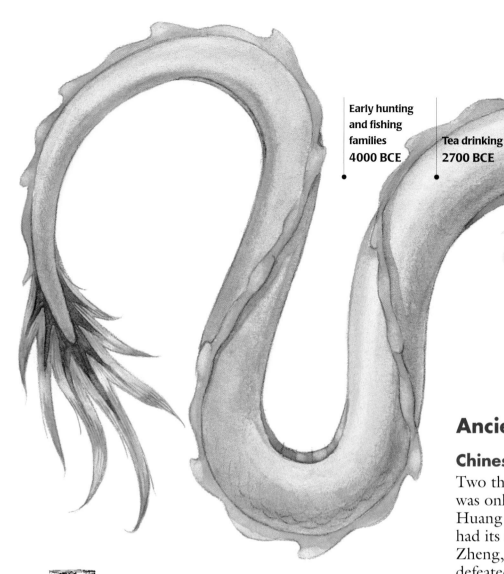

Early hunting
and fishing
families
4000 BCE

Tea drinking
2700 BCE

Silk discovered
2500 BCE

1760 BCE
Bronze weapons,
horse-drawn
chariots

Ancient China

Chinese Emperors

Two thousand years ago China was only a few small states along the Huang He (Yellow River). Each state had its own king. In 221 BCE, King Zheng, the powerful ruler of one state, defeated the other states and joined them into one kingdom. He named his new kingdom Qin (pronounced Ch'in) after the first small state he had ruled. Some historians think this was the beginning of the name China. Emperors ruled China for 2000 years. The last emperor, Pu Yi, gave up his title in 1912.

The Chinese Peasants

Farming has always been the main way of life, and the **peasants** have always been the largest group of people in China. Although the peasants did the important job of growing food, most peasants lived a difficult life. In old China the farmlands were owned by wealthy landowners. Peasants paid large **rents** to the land-owners for permission to use the land. After a year of working in the fields, peasants were sometimes left with barely enough food to feed their families.

HISTORY

For hundreds of years the emperors of China have built their palaces and temples in and around Beijing. Today many of the ancient buildings and temples have been rebuilt so they look as they did in the days of the emperors.

BOTTOM LEFT: Ancient Chinese money was made of bronze in unusual shapes.

BCE—Before the Common Era, equivalent to BC, identifies dates before the birth of Christ. Common Era, equivalent to AD, identifies historical dates after the birth of Christ.
NOTE: timeline not to scale

peasants—rural workers or farmers
rents—a portion of the crop given to the landowner as payment for using the land

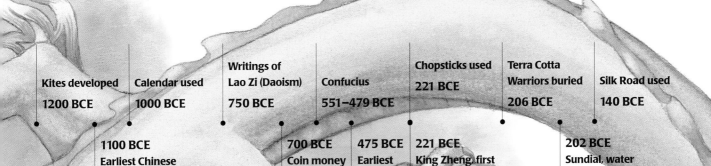

Kites developed	Calendar used	Writings of Lao Zi (Daoism)	Confucius	Chopsticks used	Terra Cotta Warriors buried	Silk Road used
1200 BCE	1000 BCE	750 BCE	551–479 BCE	221 BCE	206 BCE	140 BCE

1100 BCE
Earliest Chinese writing, bamboo books

700 BCE
Coin money produced

475 BCE
Earliest magnetic compass

221 BCE
King Zheng, first emperor of China, Great Wall begun

202 BCE
Sundial, water clock

The Forbidden City

The Forbidden City was the home of the Chinese emperors for 500 years. It was surrounded by a high wall and a deep **moat**. Soldiers guarded the entrances. The palace was called the Forbidden City because no ordinary citizen could enter the palace or even approach the walls. Only very important people were allowed inside the Forbidden City. The most well-guarded sections of the Forbidden City were the private gardens, courtyards, and apartments of the emperor and his family. Today the Forbidden City is a popular site for tourists to visit.

moat—a deep water-filled ditch

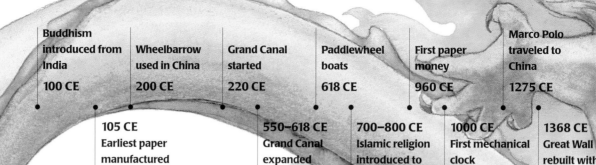

Buddhism introduced from India	Wheelbarrow used in China	Grand Canal started	Paddlewheel boats	First paper money	Marco Polo traveled to China
100 CE	200 CE	220 CE	618 CE	960 CE	1275 CE

| | 105 CE Earliest paper manufactured | | 550–618 CE Grand Canal expanded | 700–800 CE Islamic religion introduced to China | 1000 CE First mechanical clock | 1368 CE Great Wall rebuilt with stone and brick |

The Summer Palace

The Summer Palace is a group of temples and palaces built along the shore of an artificial lake outside Beijing. The emperors and their families came to the Summer Palace because it was cooler than Beijing.

Today, residents of Beijing and Chinese tourists come to the Summer Palace to avoid the heat of the city. As many as 100 000 people may visit on a summer day. Families come to enjoy the historic buildings, to picnic in the gardens, or to enjoy a paddle on the cool lake.

The Temple of Heaven

Each spring the emperor went to the Temple of Heaven to welcome the new season and to pray for good weather and good harvests.

ABOVE: Bronze drinking cup from Ancient China

RIGHT: Four views of the Summer Palace

BOTTOM LEFT: A visit to the Temple of Heaven

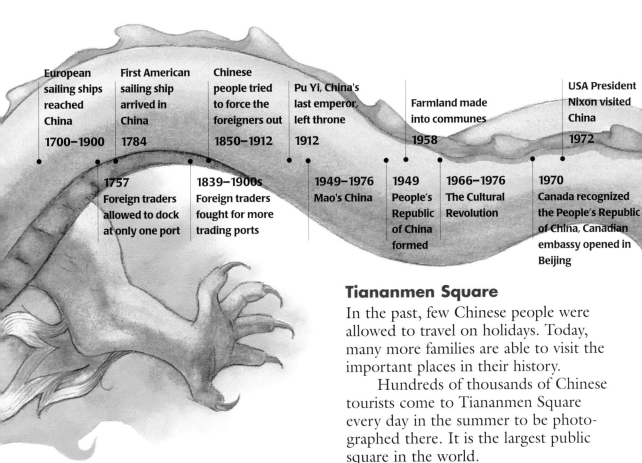

European sailing ships reached China

1700–1900

First American sailing ship arrived in China

1784

1757 Foreign traders allowed to dock at only one port

Chinese people tried to force the foreigners out

1850–1912

1839–1900s Foreign traders fought for more trading ports

Pu Yi, China's last emperor, left throne

1912

1949–1976 Mao's China

1949 People's Republic of China formed

Farmland made into communes

1958

1966–1976 The Cultural Revolution

USA President Nixon visited China

1972

1970 Canada recognized the People's Republic of China, Canadian embassy opened in Beijing

1976 Mao Zedong died

Mao's China

In 1949 the Chinese **Communist** Party, under the leadership of Mao Zedong, took control of the government. The new government believed they must improve the lives of the peasants. To accomplish that goal the government made many changes in **rural** communities. Mao's influence was enormous. His writings, contained in a small red-covered book, became the basis for everyday life in China.

Mao's ideas determined how people worked and lived. Mao Zedong so influenced the thinking of the Chinese people that the period from 1949 to 1976 is often called Mao's China.

Tiananmen Gate

Situated in front of the Forbidden City is Tiananmen Gate. Tiananmen is Chinese for "Gate of Heavenly Peace." It is used for important announcements. On October 1, 1949, Mao Zedong announced the founding of the People's Republic of China from Tiananmen Gate. Today, a portrait of Mao Zedong hangs on Tiananmen Gate.

Communist —a political system where the resources of the country are shared equally by all the people
rural—in the countryside

Tiananmen Square

In the past, few Chinese people were allowed to travel on holidays. Today, many more families are able to visit the important places in their history.

Hundreds of thousands of Chinese tourists come to Tiananmen Square every day in the summer to be photographed there. It is the largest public square in the world.

MIDDLE RIGHT: Tourists in Tiananmen Square

BOTTOM RIGHT: Portrait of Mao Zedong above Tiananmen Gate

BELOW: A "Chairman Mao" cap, with its red star pin

BEIJING, THE CAPITAL

23

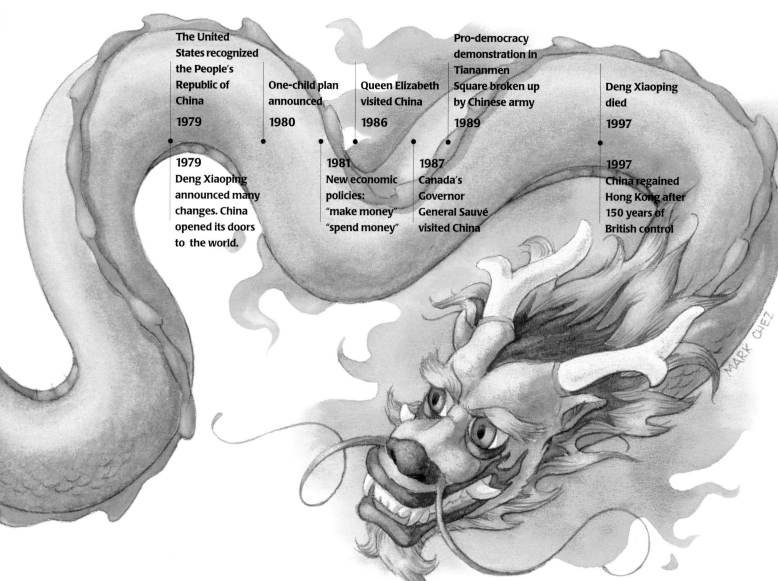

The United States recognized the People's Republic of China

1979

One-child plan announced

1980

Queen Elizabeth visited China

1986

Pro-democracy demonstration in Tiananmen Square broken up by Chinese army

1989

Deng Xiaoping died

1997

1979 Deng Xiaoping announced many changes. China opened its doors to the world.

1981 New economic policies: "make money" "spend money"

1987 Canada's Governor General Sauvé visited China

1997 China regained Hong Kong after 150 years of British control

Deng Xiaoping's China

Deng Xiaoping became the leader of China's government after Mao died in 1976. Deng Xiaoping introduced two new plans called the **open policy** and the **responsibility system** that changed life in many ways.

The open policy allowed China to trade with other countries. Foreign goods were allowed into China. Foreign companies were encouraged to build new factories in China and to start new businesses with Chinese partners. Tourists were permitted to visit. A few Chinese people were allowed to study and work outside their country.

The responsibility system allowed people to start their own businesses to make extra money. In the past, workers were assigned jobs by the government and paid the same no matter how hard they worked. With the responsibility system, the government wanted people to be responsible for their own jobs and incomes. The government encouraged people to "work hard and get rich." There were many changes under Deng Xiaoping's leadership. Deng Xiaoping died in 1997.

China Today

The goal of Mao Zedong and Deng Xiaoping was to improve the life of the Chinese people. China faces many challenges as it continues to work to achieve its goals.

---

open policy—a government plan that allowed exchange of goods, ideas, and people between China and other countries
responsibility system—a plan allowing people to work for themselves and make extra money

The Great Wall

The Great Wall of China is an amazing stone wall stretching across northern China. The Chinese often think of the Great Wall as a stone dragon with its mouth licking the Yellow Sea and its tail stretching into the Gobi Desert.

The Chinese government estimates that if all the twists and turns of the main wall and its many branches were straightened out, the Great Wall would measure 6000 kilometers. This is more than the distance across North America. The Great Wall is considered one of the greatest engineering jobs of the ancient world.

A VISIT TO THE GREAT WALL

ABOVE: Terra cotta models of Ancient Chinese soldiers.

BEIJING, THE CAPITAL

26

It was raining lightly when Taylor and her Aunt Heather arrived at the Great Wall. All Taylor could see through the steamy bus window was swirling mist. Occasionally, an outline of the treeless hills appeared through the mist.

From the bus parking lot Taylor and her aunt followed the crowds past the stalls selling pop, snacks, and T-shirts. At one of the new souvenir stalls Aunt Heather bought Taylor a small wooden model of a crossbow. It was just like the crossbows used by soldiers hundreds of years ago patrolling the Great Wall.

Taylor and Aunt Heather handed in their tickets and climbed up the stone steps. The wall was higher than Taylor expected—nearly eight meters high.

"Too bad it's raining and so misty," muttered Taylor's aunt. "We won't get any good photographs today." It was true. In both directions the wall disappeared into swirling rain clouds. Despite the poor weather, the stone walkway was crowded with tourists. Everyone seemed in a holiday mood. Groups of wet Chinese and foreign tourists laughed as they posed for pictures or bargained for a good price on T-shirts and souvenirs. Taylor wanted them all to leave so she could imagine the Great Wall as it was long ago.

Standing on her tiptoes, Taylor leaned out the archer's peephole cut into the wall. The Great Wall looked like a stone dragon lying along the spine of the hills. At a distance a lonely watchtower stood on a high ridge with clouds swirling around it. That was where Taylor wanted to go.

Taylor's aunt was setting up her video camera and tripod to get photographs of the Chinese families on the wall. In the past, mainly foreign tourists visited the wall. Today more Chinese families have money for a holiday. The shorter work week also gives workers time to take day trips with their families.

Seeing Taylor's impatient face, Aunt Heather called out, "You go on ahead, Taylor, but be careful. The walkway is very steep and it will be slippery in this rain."

Taylor trudged up the huge steps toward the farthest watchtower. It was a tough climb. In some places the steps were so high and narrow she could barely raise her leg up to the next step.

Near the top, Taylor leaned against the wall to catch her breath. Aunt Heather had told her stories about the soldiers patrolling the wall. It must have been terribly cold in the winter. Even on this summer day Taylor could feel the cold fingers of wind digging at her jacket. She wished she had her baseball hat but she'd left it in the bus. Already her face and hair were soaked from the mist.

Suddenly the watchtower appeared a short distance in front of her. She could no longer hear the laughter of other tourists trudging up the steep steps. She heard only the wet winds sweeping across the hills. She fingered the souvenir crossbow in her hands and climbed to the doorway of the watchtower.

Taylor stepped into a cold, bare stone room and moved toward the wooden ladder in the center. She imagined she could smell the smoky odor of a coal fire and the sweaty warmth of horses.

As the mist swept into the room, it seemed to Taylor that she heard the muffled knocking of hooves on stone. She imagined she saw sacks of grain piled up in the dark corners of the watchtower. In ancient times these watchtowers had held horses, soldiers, supplies, and ammunition.

Aunt Heather had told Taylor about soldiers who lived their entire lives from childhood to old age on the wall. When they died they were buried near it. Some people believed they still patrolled the wall. Taylor shivered and scurried quickly up the ladder.

The lookout was high enough to be almost above the clouds and mists. For a moment Taylor could see the other branch of the wall climbing the far ridges. Then it vanished again into the clouds.

It was easy to imagine the **invaders** riding swiftly along these ridges, hidden in thick fog.

As her eyes scanned the rocky ridges, she thought she saw black shadows move through the mists. The clouds cleared and the shadows moved to a lower ridge. Taylor clutched the crossbow. Standing on her toes she leaned far out across the thick wall. She aimed her crossbow at the silent ridges. For a few exciting moments Taylor was a soldier defending ancient China from the northern invaders.

The mists came closer and the ridges disappeared. Nothing moved. Eventually Taylor recalled that she was a tourist on holiday.

Smiling to herself and tucking her hands into her warm pockets, she started the long walk back down the wall. The steps were so steep and narrow that hiking back down was almost as difficult as the climb up.

When Taylor reached her aunt she was still smiling. "This is such a miserable day to come to the Great Wall," Aunt Heather exclaimed. "I thought you'd be disappointed that you didn't see anything."

Taylor smiled broadly. "It was a wonderful trip to the Great Wall. It was perfect weather for seeing."

invaders—people who take over by force

Green Learning Academy
www.greenlearning.com
(403) 873-1966
Calgary, Alberta

People's Republic of China

GOVERNMENT

Beijing is China's capital city. The government of China meets here. Since October 1, 1949, the government has been controlled by the Chinese Communist Party.

The Chinese Communist Party believes in communism. Communists believe that a country's resources should benefit all the people. Under a communist system the needs of all people are provided by the government. The Chinese communist government tried to provide food, a place to live, education, health care, clothing, and jobs for everyone.

In the past, the communist government gave individuals very little say in the ways they were governed. People did not have a chance to vote. People also had few choices in their daily lives. The government decided what crops were grown, what goods were produced by factories, where people lived, what jobs people had, what style of clothing people wore, and how many children a couple had.

In recent years, the Chinese government has given people more choices and **freedoms** in their daily lives. However, the Chinese Communist Party still controls the government and much of people's lives. People do have an opportunity to vote, but the Communist Party must approve the **candidates**.

Tiananmen Square Incident

In 1989 some people began to express dissatisfaction with the type of government in China. Some of these people, especially university students in Beijing, wanted China to become a **democracy**. A democracy is a **political** system where people vote for government members and have a say in government decision making. Also in a democracy, individuals have many rights and freedoms.

In April of 1989 thousands of students organized a **demonstration** in Tiananmen Square supporting the idea of democracy for China. Students camped out in the square for two months. They made speeches favoring democracy.

On June 4 the government ordered the army to break up the democracy demonstrations. Tanks rolled into Tiananmen Square. Soldiers fired on students and other demonstrators. Hundreds were killed. Some student leaders were sent to prison and others were executed. A few escaped to North America. While the Chinese government was prepared to allow people more freedoms and choices about making a living and lifestyles, they would not allow changes to the political system.

Major political gatherings are held in the Great Hall of the People, which is beside Tiananmen Square.

freedoms—the power to make choices for oneself
candidates—people who are seeking a position or office

political—providing direction, order, and security to meet group needs
demonstration—a public meeting to express an opinion on an issue

TRADE

Beijing is an important trade center for China. Trade is the exchange of goods between countries. Canada and the United States, for example, buy from other countries to get goods they want but do not usually produce themselves or which are less costly. Canadian and American companies also sell goods to other countries to make money.

Government and company officials from around the world come to Beijing to arrange trade agreements. These trade officials try to organize opportunities for companies from their country to do business in China. The countries of the Pacific Rim are important to each other for trade and business. North American companies hope to sell their goods and products to the millions of people in China. They also buy goods produced in China. Each year the value of trade between North America and China increases.

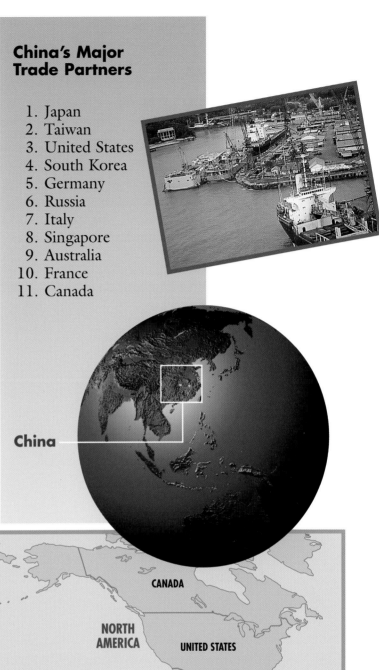

China's Major Trade Partners

1. Japan
2. Taiwan
3. United States
4. South Korea
5. Germany
6. Russia
7. Italy
8. Singapore
9. Australia
10. France
11. Canada

China

China in the Pacific Rim

RUSSIA

ASIA

CANADA

NORTH AMERICA

NORTH KOREA

JAPAN

CHINA

UNITED STATES

SOUTH KOREA

TAIWAN

MEXICO

PHILIPPINES

MALAYSIA

SINGAPORE

INDONESIA

Pacific Ocean

COLOMBIA

ECUADOR

PERU

N

AUSTRALIA

W   E

SOUTH AMERICA

S

CHILE

NEW ZEALAND

0   2000 km

LOOKING BACK

Activities

Geography of North China (pages 10–13)

1. On a world map **compare** the latitude positions of Beijing and Harbin or Daqing with places in North America. **List** similarities and differences of climate and seasons you would expect to find, based on latitude position.

2. **List** examples of how the geography of North China affects how people meet their basic needs.

> Needs are basic human requirements for survival.
>
> People have physical, psychological, and group (social) needs.

> Wants are things you desire or that you think can be used to satisfy a need. Wants are learned.
>
> People have physical, psychological, and group (social) wants.

3. ➡ As you work through the text, **create** a large geography map of China. Use the Regions of China map on the inside back cover of the text and enlarge it onto a poster-size sheet. Transfer the three region boundaries onto it, then use information from pages 10–12, the mini-atlas at the back of the book, and your atlas to add the following to the North China region:
   a) **Mark** or **glue** on it:
   - Huang He, North China Plain, Northeast China Plain, Beijing, Harbin, Xian, Daqing, plus 10 other cities
   - areas where the following are grown or located: wheat, corn, soybeans, cattle, pigs, hydro-electric power, oil, timber
   b) **Draw** people to represent the population of North China on a pictorial (using pictures) graph of the population of China. Leave room for the populations of West and South China. Place your graph at the bottom of your map.
   c) **Add** a key to your map, a compass rose, a title, and a scale.

Getting Around (pages 14–17)

1. Look through magazines and newspapers. **Cut out** advertisements for North American transportation vehicles and transportation systems. Make a **chart display** of your collection. Make a **list** of the transportation used in China. Are there similarities or differences?

2. **Write** two paragraphs describing some problems that might occur if more people in China could afford to own automobiles. Are there forms of Chinese transportation that would be useful in solving traffic problems in crowded North American cities?

Living in the City (pages 18–19)

1. **Write** a paragraph describing how people in Beijing meet their housing needs.

2. From newspaper advertisements **cut out** examples that show different types of urban housing. Check the amount of floor space offered in these homes. Use a comparison chart to **compare** North American city homes and Chinese city homes. Comparison charts are explained on page 146.

3. **Construct** a model or a diorama of a courtyard home.

History (pages 20–27)

1. Many Chinese people are now visiting the historical sites of China.
   a) **Name** some of these sites and **write** one to two sentences describing what people see when they visit these sites.
   b) What needs are being met by visiting these historical sites?

Government (page 28)

1. Using information you have gathered about China's government, start a **web** showing how the Chinese government influences or controls the way the people live. Webs are explained on page 143.

Trade (page 29)

1. Make a **list** of reasons trade with China is important to North America.

2. Make a **list** of products in your home, school, and community which carry a Made in China label. **Evaluate** the items of your list. What do these items tell you about China's exports?

Chapter Review

1. Use one of the strategies on page 142 of the Appendix for **recording** the following vocabulary in the WordBook section of your China binder: Pacific Rim trade, export, work unit, open policy, responsibility system, freedom, government.

2. **Create** and **present** a word poster with one of the chapter's vocabulary terms. Word posters are described in the Appendix on page 144.

3. a) **Record** what steps one goes through to classify information. Check your answer with page 145.
   b) **Look** carefully at the photographs in this chapter. From the information in the photographs, **list** and then **classify** into two categories the ways Chinese people meet their needs and wants.
   c) Sub-divide your classification of needs and wants into
   - physical, psychological, and group needs
   - physical, psychological, and group wants

4. **Check** the organization of your activities for this chapter in your binder:
   - chapter title page, notes, activities, maps, and illustrations in Activities section
   - definitions in WordBook section
   - China Journal writings
   - Tools of Learning notes

5. Do either a) or b).
   a) **Summarize** your research notes for this chapter into a retrieval chart. Either make your own chart (see page 144 in the Appendix) or ask your teacher for a summary chart for this chapter.
   b) **Answer** Taylor's questions on page 7.

6. When you have finished reading about Taylor's visit to Beijing, **write** your own captions for the photographs on pages 8–9. Do not write in the textbook. Include information from what you learned in the chapter.

7. Imagine you are with Taylor and you are sending a message home to family or friends. **Create** a set of postcards from Beijing. **Draw** a picture on one side of the postcard highlighting a place of interest. **Write** a message on the reverse side describing the scene or some experience you had in China. Include three facts and three impressions or personal feelings. You may prepare a letter or an e-mail message instead of a postcard.

8. **Create** a game about Beijing. Include at least 10 facts in it.

9. **Create** a travel brochure encouraging North Americans to visit Beijing.

Grasslands, Desert, and Mountains

Inner Mongolian Grasslands

Urumqi

Northwest Desert

•Hohot
Beijing★

Tibetan Plateau

•Lhasa

Mongolian—associated with the Mongol peoples of Mongolia and Inner Mongolia

environment—the air, land, and water that we share with all living and non-living things

desert—an area of low rainfall, often less than 200 mm

yurt—a round tent made from animal hides

caravan—a group of people traveling with pack horses, camels, or donkeys

Here we are at the Beijing airport waiting to start our tour of West China. I think we're going to be spending a lot of time flying and waiting in airports on this part of our trip. West China is a huge region! My map shows the places we will be visiting. The West China region includes the Inner Mongolian Grasslands, the Northwest Desert, and the Tibetan Plateau.

The environment in West China makes it very difficult for people to meet their needs. West China has both extremely high, snow covered mountains and dry, scorching desert areas. Aunt Heather has given me a copy of her geography notes. She has visited many areas of West China on previous trips.

First, we will fly to Hohot in Inner Mongolia and take a three-day bus trip through the grasslands. Instead of hotels we'll stay in traditional Mongolian tent houses called yurts. Aunt Heather showed me a photograph of a yurt she stayed in on her last trip. I didn't expect to be camping in China. This should be fun!

After Hohot we will fly to Urumqi in the Northwest. The Northwest is mainly areas of sand and gravel desert. Aunt Heather said the sand dunes in some places are higher than a house! She also said that some of the hottest temperatures on earth were recorded in the Northwest Desert. I hope it won't be that hot while we're there!

From Urumqi we will visit several cities on the Silk Road. In ancient times the only route to China from Europe and the Middle East was a trail winding across the snowcapped mountains and desert of the Northwest. Camel caravans used this trail to carry silk from China to Europe. This trail became known as the Silk Road.

Aunt Heather told me that the method for making silk was just one of the great discoveries made in China. I've started a section in my journal for

Chinese inventions and discoveries. I was surprised when she told me the Chinese invented ice cream and nail polish.

From Urumqi we'll fly to Lhasa in Tibet. Tibet is part of the Tibetan Plateau, which stretches over a large area of West China. Tibet is often called the "roof of the world" because the mountains are so high. Aunt Heather says we may feel dizzy and have trouble breathing there. Lhasa is so high there is less oxygen in the air. It's also going to be very chilly because of the high elevation. Beijing has been so hot—it's hard to believe I might soon need my fleece jacket.

I'm really looking forward to seeing some of China's minority nationality peoples on this trip. My guide book says over 92% of the population is Han Chinese. The other people belong to 55 minority nationalities. Most of China's minority nationalities live in West China. Each minority group has its own style of clothing, language, and customs.

This will be a great opportunity for me to research people's beliefs in China. The many different nationalities follow several different religions and systems of beliefs.

Aunt Heather told me that we are fortunate to be able to make this tour through West China. When she first came here it was difficult to travel through that region because there were very few roads, railways, or airports. In the past it might have taken several months to make the trip we will do in a few days by plane.

I'm glad there are new airports today so we can see West China, but I don't like waiting. I wish they would call us for our flight! This is going to be a great trip. I want to get started!

草原，沙漠，山川

What I want to find out in West China:
1. How does the geography of West China affect how people meet their needs?
2. What is life like on the grasslands?
3. What is life like in the Northwest Desert?
4. What is life like on the Tibetan Plateau?
5. Who are China's minority nationalities?
6. What kinds of beliefs are followed in China?
7. What are some of the great discoveries and inventions made in China?

GEOGRAPHY OF WEST CHINA

The West region includes the Inner Mongolian Grasslands, the Northwest Desert, and the Tibetan Plateau. The region covers 53% of China's land area, but less than 5% of China's population lives there. The environment is very difficult. West China includes some of the hottest, driest desert areas and some of the highest mountains in the world.

1

53% of China's land area is in West China

5% of China's population lives in West China

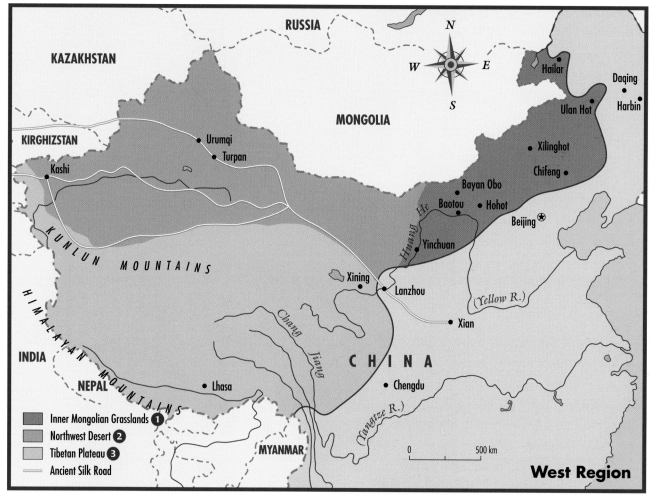

RUSSIA

KAZAKHSTAN

N
W — E
S

Hailar

Daqing
Ulan Hot • Harbin

MONGOLIA

KIRGHIZSTAN
Urumqi •
Turpan •

Xilinghot •

Chifeng •

Kashi •

Bayan Obo •
Baotou • Hohot •

Beijing ✲

K U N L U N   M O U N T A I N S

Yinchuan •

Xining •
Lanzhou •

(Yellow R.)

H I M A L A Y A N   M O U N T A I N S

Chang Jiang

Xian •

C H I N A

INDIA

NEPAL
Lhasa •

Chengdu •

■ Inner Mongolian Grasslands ❶
■ Northwest Desert ❷
■ Tibetan Plateau ❸
Ancient Silk Road

(Yangtze R.)

MYANMAR

0   500 km

West Region

2

3

INNER MONGOLIAN GRASSLANDS

Landforms

- hills and plateaus
- small areas of desert

Rivers

- few rivers
- rivers shallow; often dry up

Climate

- short, warm summers
- dry; drought a problem
- sometimes no rain for 12 months then sudden heavy rainstorms
- great variation in temperature between night and day in summer (fur coats at night, light clothes during the day)
- long, cold winters; often heavy snowfalls
- strong winds all year

Agriculture

- limited agriculture
- **irrigation** usually necessary; use water from Huang He (Yellow River)
- one crop a year; main crops: winter wheat, oats, corn, sorghum, millet, potatoes, **flax**, and **canola**
- main activity is raising sheep, goats, horses, cattle, donkeys, pigs, and camels

| Winter Wheat | Sheep | Horse |

Natural Resources

- copper, coal, iron, gold, and lead deposits

Transportation

- horses, camels, trucks
- more highways and railway lines built, but still few in number
- new airline services connect cities of Hohot and Yinchuan to Beijing

Population

- small population
- a few cities; mainly scattered villages
- Han Chinese and several minority nationalities (Mongolian and Hui peoples are the largest minorities)

irrigation—a constant source of water supplied through ditches or channels
flax—a blue-flowered plant used to make linseed oil and linen cloth
canola—a plant grown for oil made from seeds

BUS TRIP TO THE GRASSLANDS

We spent a busy day in Hohot. We toured both a Buddhist temple and an Islamic mosque there. These religious buildings seemed very different from churches I am used to at home. Then we set off on a three-day bus trip through Inner Mongolia to see the grasslands.

The grasslands remind me of North American plains. There are few trees. The rolling hills are covered with emerald-green grasses. We passed many large herds of cattle, sheep, and goats. Horses grazed on the wild grasses.

The last two nights we stayed at Mongolian settlements and slept in yurts. The yurts had no corners, only round, soft walls. The walls came only to my shoulders. I had to bend down to go through the doorway but it was high enough in the middle for me to stand up. The beds were thick rugs spread on a woven mat floor.

In the evening we sat on cushions around a small charcoal stove and ate a Mongolian meal of lamb, goat cheese, and tea with horse's milk. Even with a

chilly wind blowing outside, the yurt was pleasantly warm. It felt just like camping at home except we didn't need to worry about bears!

A yurt is a practical home for families on the grasslands. When a family moves their herd to another area, the yurt is folded, packed into a wagon or truck, and set up in a new location. In the past, people used camels and horses for transportation. Today trucks are more common.

The grasslands seem so empty compared to Beijing. Aunt Heather said there are only a few large cities in the Inner Mongolian grasslands. Since leaving Hohot we've seen only a few small villages. In the past herding families moved their cattle and sheep to new pastures every few months. People did not stay in one place for very long. That's why there are so few villages and towns on the grasslands.

Today life on the grasslands is changing. Herding families are building special fenced-in areas for their cattle.

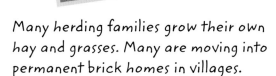

Many herding families grow their own hay and grasses. Many are moving into permanent brick homes in villages.

Yesterday we were lucky to be at a village for a gathering of families. Herding families like to meet several times a year. They hold wrestling matches and race their horses and camels.

After the races I got to ride a camel! It swayed so much I felt seasick after only a few minutes.

It's cooler on the grasslands than it was in Beijing. Even though it's summer, I need a sweater in the morning and a warm jacket at night. It felt like autumn days at home. They have cold, snowy winters here. Many things about life on the grasslands remind me of home and make me feel a little homesick.

NORTHWEST DESERT

Landforms
- vast areas of sand and gravel desert
- mountains, plateaus, and **basins**

Rivers
- shallow rivers; sometimes dry up
- rivers important sources of irrigation water for farming

Climate
- China's desert areas among the driest and hottest in the world
- extremes of temperatures from summer to winter
- hot, dry summers (hot during day, cold at night)
- low **precipitation**
- sometimes no rain for six months then sudden, heavy rainstorms
- long, cold winters
- China's highest temperature (47.6°C) recorded at Turpan in Northwest; China's lowest temperature (−51.5°C) recorded just north of Turpan
- strong winds all year

basins—areas of low land surrounded by higher land
precipitation—rain or snow falling to the ground
oasis—a fertile spot in the desert with a water source
nomadic herders—people who keep herds of animals and travel to find new areas of grazing land for their animals

Agriculture
- mainly **oasis** farming
- good soil but limited water resources
- irrigation has increased amount of land used for farming
- one crop a year; main crops: winter wheat, oats, potatoes, flax, and canola
- many people are **nomadic herders**; goats, sheep, camels raised

Natural Resources
- largest nickel and copper deposits in China
- large oil, coal, iron, and gold deposits
- hydroelectric stations on mountain rivers
- forestry resources in mountains

Transportation
- camels, trucks
- new highways and railway lines built
- new airline services connect oasis cities to Beijing

Population
- low population
- few large cities; mainly scattered villages and small towns
- large number of minority nationality groups (Uygur minority nationality makes up nearly half the population)

ANCIENT OASIS CITIES

We have been so busy since we arrived in Urumqi I haven't had much time to work on my journal. The Northwest is unbelievable! This part of China has huge gravel and sand desert areas surrounded by high snow-covered mountains. We've traveled to many fascinating places this week.

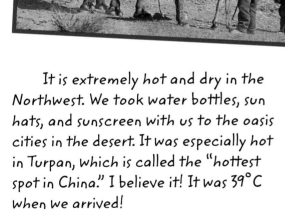

A smiling Buddha

It is extremely hot and dry in the Northwest. We took water bottles, sun hats, and sunscreen with us to the oasis cities in the desert. It was especially hot in Turpan, which is called the "hottest spot in China." I believe it! It was 39°C when we arrived!

Turpan is a large city surrounded by grain fields. Turpan gets its water from wells and underground water channels dug 2000 years ago. The water comes from melting snow in the nearby mountains. Hundreds of years ago the oasis cities were caravan stops along the ancient Silk Road between China and Europe. Today many of them are centers of agriculture and new industries.

While we were in Turpan we took a minibus trip into the desert. We saw a place where a thousand statues of the Buddha were once carved into the walls of caves. Most of the statues are gone now. The Buddhist religion was brought to China by traders from India hundreds of years ago.

Islam is a religion that was introduced to China from the Middle East. It came to China with traders on the Silk Road. Many of the minority nationalities in the Northwest follow Islam. Urumqi and Turpan both have beautiful mosques where these people worship.

Marco Polo—European trader who traveled to China around 1275

Yesterday we flew to Kashi, another ancient city on the Silk Road. Kashi is famous for its bazaar. There have been bazaars in Kashi for over a thousand years. Marco Polo stopped here on his journey to China. He wrote about the bazaar in his journal.

The bazaar was an amazing market of food and goods. Covered stalls sold handmade boots, decorated knives, the brightly colored skirts and scarves the women here wear, embroidered caps, fur-lined headgear, painted wooden saddles, fruit, vegetables, meat, live goats, and lots of interesting foods. The melons and the bread that looked like bagels were delicious! Aunt Heather bought big bags of raisins and peanuts for our trips to the desert.

Nearly everyone at the Kashi bazaar belonged to a minority nationality. At least 13 minority nationalities live in the Northwest. The largest groups are the Uygur, Kirghiz, and Kazakh peoples.

Aunt Heather is going to take me to the museum in Urumqi. I will research more about the minority nationalities and different beliefs in China. I want to include a section on these in my journal.

There is so much to learn about life in China. I don't think I brought a big enough journal!

TIBETAN PLATEAU

Landforms
- some of the highest mountains in world, snow-covered year round
- highest plateaus in the world
- hills

Rivers
- many long rivers such as Huang He and Chang Jiang start in mountains
- largest number of lakes in China

Climate

- high elevation
- low temperatures all year
- long, cold winters, often with snow
- great differences between day and night temperatures or sunny and shady places
- strong winds all year
- precipitation varies throughout region

Agriculture
- limited agriculture; mainly in valleys
- irrigation needed in many areas
- one crop a year; main crops: winter wheat, barley, potatoes, peas, flax, and canola; corn and sugar beets grown in drier areas
- many people are nomadic herders; sheep, goats, **yaks** raised

Winter Wheat   Sheep   Yak

Natural Resources
- hydroelectric stations on rivers
- large forest resources
- oil deposits
- mining of salt, potassium, and other minerals

Transportation
- yaks, trucks
- one railway
- few roads; most unpaved, gravel
- new air routes

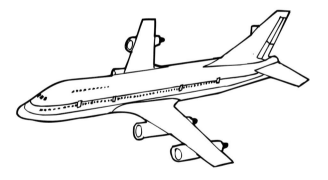

Population
- low population
- few cities
- Population: 60% Han Chinese
- Tibetans are a large minority nationality

yaks—long-haired oxen of Tibet

TIBET ADVENTURE

I felt the effects of Lhasa's high elevation as soon as we landed. By the time we collected our luggage I had a headache and felt dizzy. Luckily there was an oxygen bag in the taxi we took to our hotel. I felt much better

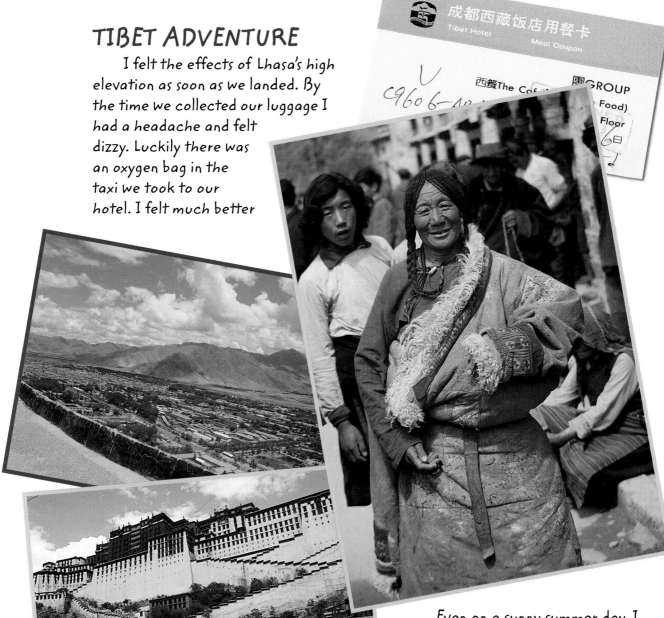

after a few deep gulps of oxygen. We will be taking it easy for the first few days until we adjust to the high elevation and low oxygen.

I was glad to rest at the hotel and look at the maps in my guide book. The Tibetan Plateau covers a really large area of West China. Tibet is only one part of the plateau.

Aunt Heather showed me a satellite photograph of China. It really shows the high mountains.

Even on a sunny summer day, I thought Lhasa was very chilly. I was glad I had my fleece jacket. Everyone seemed to be wearing warm clothes. Many people wore long, wrap-around robes tied at the waist. Some wore woolen hats and had scarves around their necks. After the heat of the desert this was quite a change. It was hard to believe the grasslands, the desert, and these high mountains are in the same country.

Aunt Heather took me to see the Potala Palace. The Potala Palace was once the center of the Tibetan government and religion. The Tibetan religion is a form of Buddhism.

The palace was amazing. It seemed to be carved right out of the rocky mountain slope. Aunt Heather said the

steep steps up to the Potala would be too tough a climb for our first day in Lhasa. We can tour the Palace in a few days, after we've adjusted to the high elevation.

I really enjoyed the market in Lhasa. There were very few vegetables and fruit for sale, but lots of dried yak meat and warm woolen clothing. I bought an embroidered woolen hat and a pair of gloves. My guide book says temperatures in Lhasa can drop below freezing at night, even in the summer.

It was two days before I adjusted to the high elevation and felt well enough to travel into the countryside. Roads here are mainly gravel or dirt. It was a very dusty trip, but the scenery was spectacular! I've never seen such high, snow-covered mountains.

There are lots of rivers and streams, but the land seems very dry. I don't think it rains here often. We passed many areas of gravel plains with no vegetation.

We saw no farms or houses that day. We did pass several herding families with their ponies and yaks. All their possessions were in bundles and bags tied to the yaks. Aunt Heather says that yaks provide all the basic needs for the Tibetan people. The animals supply milk and meat. The wool and hides are used for clothing and to make the traditional tents. Yaks are also used for transportation.

Yesterday we stopped at the campsite of a herding family. Their tent was similar to the yurts we stayed in on the grasslands. It was brown because it was made of yak wool. The family served us noodles, dried yak meat, and yak-butter tea.

Even after all the traveling, we have seen only a small part of the West region. I'd love to come back and see more of the West, but I'll remember to bring warmer clothes next time.

8% of China's population belongs to the 55 minority nationalities.

Five Autonomous Regions
1. Nei Mongol (Inner Mongolia)
2. Xizang (Tibet)
3. Xinjiang
4. Ningxia
5. Guangxi

ABOVE: When North Americans think about Chinese people they usually think about Han, because most Chinese people are Han.

MINORITY NATIONALITIES

Most of China's population is Han Chinese. They are the largest group in China. A small part of the total population belongs to China's 55 minority nationalities. These are groups that have their own language and culture (way of life).

There are only a few thousand people in some Chinese minority groups. Others have populations of several million. The Tibetans are one of China's largest minorities.

Most minority groups live in China's five **autonomous regions**. These regions are mainly along China's borders.

An autonomous region is allowed some self-government. The region does not have to follow all the laws decided by the Chinese government. People are allowed to keep their own languages, customs, and traditions.

Each minority has its own style of clothing and housing. Groups have their own languages, foods, customs, and festivals. Minorities follow Islam, Buddhism, or their own particular beliefs.

MARK CHEZ

GRASSLANDS, DESERT, AND MOUNTAINS

44

©1995 DENNIS COX/CHINASTOCK

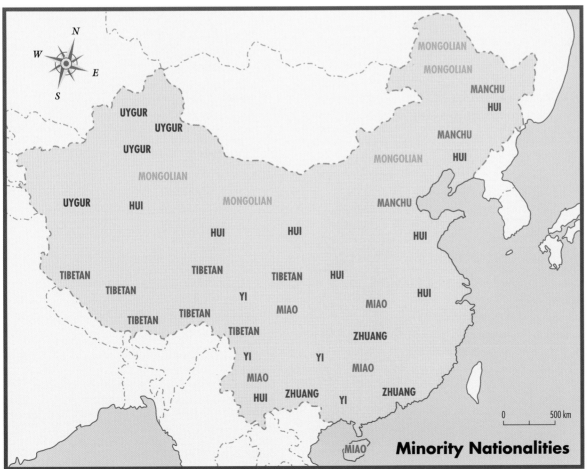

Some Minority Nationalities

1 Mongolian
2 Tibetan
3 Uygur
4 Hui
5 Miao

Map showing where the largest groups of minority nationalities live.

Minority Nationalities

0 — 500 km

BELIEFS

Over the centuries Chinese people have held many different beliefs. Several sets of beliefs originated in China. Others came there through trade and contact with other cultures. The government today does not encourage religious activities. There is, however, a growing interest in them.

Ancestor Worship

Ancestor worship was practiced in China for thousands of years. People made offerings of food to the spirits of the ancestors on an **altar** in the family home or a **temple**. They believed that showing respect for the spirits of their ancestors would bring them good fortune. Respect for ancestors is still valued in China today.

Confucius

Confucius was a great thinker and writer who lived in ancient China. He developed ideas about how people should behave so there would be social **harmony**. His ideas influenced life in China for more than 2000 years. Confucius taught that everyone had a place in **society** with duties and responsibilities.

Confucius believed the family was very important. Ancestors were honored. Children were taught to obey their parents, respect older family members, and obey the rulers of the country. Confucian **values** are still held by many people in China.

ABOVE: Kuan Yin was an Ancient Chinese goddess.
BOTTOM LEFT: Two Ancient Chinese thinkers playing a board game.

Confucius said

*To make a mistake and not correct it: this is a **real** mistake.*

If everybody hates something, you'd better check into it; if everybody loves something, you'd better check into it.

To study and not think is a waste. To think and not study is dangerous.

Daoism

Daoism started in China. The writings of Lao Zi are recorded in an ancient book, the *Dao De Jing*. Daoism teaches respect for nature and living in harmony with nature. **Herbal** medicines, special diets, massage techniques, and exercises were developed to keep the body healthy. Today these medicines and practices are popular in many countries besides China.

From the *Dao De Jing* by Lao Zi

A thick tree grows from a tiny seed.

A journey of a thousand kilometers starts with one step.

altar—a raised place or small table used in religious ceremonies
temple—a religious building or place of worship
harmony—an agreeable, balanced state; orderliness
society—all the relationships that exist among the people of a place
values—opinions on what we believe is good or how things ought to be
herbal—related to plants or natural sources

Islam

Islam came to China with Arab traders from the Middle East. Islam teaches that there is one God. The holy book of Islam, called the **Qur'an**, recorded the teachings of the prophet Muhammad. Today Islam has a large following in China, particularly among many minority nationalities.

Christianity

Missionaries and European traders brought **Christianity** to China hundreds of years ago. The teachings of Christ are recorded in the **Bible**, the holy book of Christianity. In China, most churches are found in large cities such as Shanghai, Beijing, and Hong Kong. Christian churches, like temples and mosques, are controlled by the government.

Buddhism

Traders from India brought **Buddhism** to China. Buddhism teaches that life is a cycle of birth, death, and rebirth until a state of perfection is reached. Many Han Chinese and minority nationalities follow Buddhism.

TOP LEFT: The towers on mosques are used to call people to prayer.

BOTTOM LEFT: Church services are often held in shops or homes.

ABOVE: A laughing Buddha

TOP RIGHT: The pagoda is an impressive feature of a Buddhist temple. Pagodas were built to store religious items and documents or to celebrate special events.

BOTTOM RIGHT: Buddhists praying in a temple

Islam—religion based on teachings of the prophet Muhammad
missionaries—people who bring religious teachings to others

DISCOVERIES AND INVENTIONS

The ancient Chinese were great inventors. They developed many new ideas long before anyone else in the world thought of them. The timeline on pages 20–24 shows when many of these discoveries and inventions were made.

Chinese inventions reached other countries through trade. Several had a great impact on other cultures. The compass allowed European sailors to travel across the ocean and explore new parts of the world. Gunpowder changed warfare throughout the world. Paper making and the printing process made books available to more people. This started a new interest in reading and learning in Europe.

The mechanical clock, the crossbow, the process of **casting iron**, the umbrella, the stirrup, and a type of earthquake detector were Chinese inventions. Sometimes scholars disagree about where a discovery was made, and some inventions may have been developed in more than one place.

1 Ice cream

2 "Rocks that burned" (coal)

3 Nail polish

4 Wheelbarrow

5 Production of silk/spinning and weaving

6 Fishing reel

casting iron—heating iron to high temperatures until molten and then pouring it into molds

7 Waterwheel
8 Animal harnesses to pull wagons/carts
9 Tea drinking
10 Porcelain
11 Kites
12 Noodles
13 Fireworks
14 Rudder

porcelain—a thin china made from kaolin clay
rudder—the steering mechanism of a boat

LOOKING BACK

Activities

Geography of West China (pages 34–43)

1. On page 30 you started an on-going project on the geography of China. Use information from pages 34–43, the mini-atlas at the back of the book, and your atlas to add the following to the West China region:

   a) **Mark** or **glue** on it:
   - Hohot, Urumqi, Turpan, Kashi, Lhasa, Inner Mongolian Grasslands, Northwest Desert, Tibetan Plateau, Huang He, and Chang Jiang
   - areas where the following are grown or located: winter wheat, sheep, yaks, goats, horses, donkeys, cattle, pigs, camels, oil, salt, potassium, copper, coal, iron, gold, lead, nickel, forestry

   b) **Draw** people to represent the population of West China on your pictorial graph of the population of China. Place them near your representation of the population of North China, for comparison.

2. Using a map scale **estimate** how far Taylor and Aunt Heather traveled during their tour of West China.

Inner Mongolian Grasslands (pages 35–37)

1. Make a **chart** listing how technology has changed life on the grasslands. **Predict** how the introduction of new technology (transportation, communication, electricity, dams, and irrigation systems) might change life in future years.

2. In small groups develop a **role-play** in which each student takes the role of a member of a herding family. Hold a class **interview** where reporters ask questions of family members to find out how life on the grasslands is changing.

3. **Construct** a model or a diorama of a Mongolian yurt.

Northwest Desert (pages 38–40)

1. Make a **chart** listing how life has changed in the Northwest Desert. **Predict** how the introduction of new technology (transportation, communications, electricity, dams, and irrigation systems) might change life in future years.

2. With your class, **organize** and **put on** a bazaar similar to the one described in Taylor's journal.

3. **Construct** a mural or diorama depicting the oasis cities, religious buildings, and/or bazaar that Taylor visited.

Tibetan Plateau (Pages 41–43)

1. Make a **chart** listing examples of how life has changed on the Tibetan Plateau. **Predict** how the introduction of new technology (transportation, communication, electricity, dams, and irrigation systems) might change life in future years.

2. Develop a **role-play interview** between a North American student and a teenager from a herding family on the Tibetan Plateau. Include information on basic needs.

3. **Write** a letter describing your day with a herding family. **Illustrate** your letter with sketches.

West China (pages 34–43)

1. Make a **list** of ways the geography of the different parts of West China affects how people meet their basic needs. **Compare** similarities and differences between grasslands, desert, and mountains. Comparing is explained on page 146.

2. Refer to Presentations on page 147 and select a method to **present** ways that people in West China meet their basic needs.

Minority Nationalities (pages 44–45)

1. Select a strategy from Note Making on page 143 to **make notes** on Minority Nationalities in China.

Beliefs (pages 46–47)

1. Select a strategy from Note Making on page 143 to **make notes** on Beliefs.

2. In a few sentences **explain** what each of the sayings of Confucius and Lao Zi on page 46 is meant to teach.

3. **Create** banners with sayings of Confucius and Lao Zi for your classroom.

4. **Add** information from page 47 to your WordBook for: Islam, Buddhism.

Discoveries and Inventions (pages 48–49)

1. Which three discoveries and inventions do you consider to be China's most important contributions to the world? **Write** a few sentences explaining your reasons.

Chapter Review

1. Use one of the strategies on page 142 for **recording** the following vocabulary: minority nationalities, values. Put this assignment in the WordBook section of your China binder.

2. **Create** and **present** a word poster with one of the chapter's vocabulary terms. Word posters are described in the Appendix on page 144.

3. **Classify** the photographs in this chapter into
   • physical, psychological, and group needs
   • physical, psychological, and group wants
   Classification is explained on page 145.

4. **Check** the organization of your activities for this chapter in your binder:
   • chapter title page, notes, activities, maps, and illustrations in Activities section
   • definitions in WordBook section
   • China Journal writings
   • Tools of Learning notes

5. Do either a) or b).
   a) **Summarize** your research notes for this chapter into a retrieval chart. Either make your own chart (see page 144 in the Appendix) or ask your teacher for a summary chart for this chapter.
   b) **Answer** Taylor's questions on page 33.

6. When you have finished reading about Taylor's visit to West China, **write** your own captions for the photographs on pages 35–43. Do not write in the textbook. Include information from what you learned in the chapter.

7. **Create** a letter, postcard, illustrated poem, or story about West China describing some experience you had. Include three facts and three impressions or personal feelings.

8. **Create** one of the following about West China: board game, puzzle, skit, radio show, song, or rap. Include at least 10 facts in it.

9. Pretend your job is to encourage North Americans to visit West China. **Create** one of the following: magazine or newspaper article, pamphlet, travel brochure, or display.

10.   In question 1 on page 31 under Government you started a **web** showing how the Chinese government influences or controls the way the people live. Add information from this chapter to your web.

In the Countryside

• Chengdu

paddies—small irrigated rice fields

humid—a large amount of moisture in the air

clinic—a medical office dealing with minor illnesses or injuries

West China was wonderful. Now we will travel through the countryside and cities of South China, visiting Chengdu, Shanghai, Hong Kong, and Shenzhen. Our first stop is Chengdu.

The views from the plane as we circled Chengdu were spectacular! Green rice paddies spread in all directions. Even the steep hillsides are covered with them. Aunt Heather said farmers cut narrow steps called terraces into the hills. These make small fields for growing rice or vegetables. My guide book said Chengdu is one of the best rice growing areas in South China. This will be a good place to research rice growing and life in the countryside.

It is warm and humid in Chengdu. I'm happy to pack away my fleece jacket and wear T-shirts again. Aunt Heather says it is usually very hot and rainy here at this time of the year.

Chengdu is much bigger than I expected. The streets seem even more crowded with bicycles than Beijing. Aunt Heather was surprised by the number of new apartment buildings, office towers, department stores, and fast food restaurants built here since her visit three years ago.

Last night we walked to a nearby restaurant for dinner. We picked a hot pot restaurant because Chengdu is famous for this style of cooking. The food was cooked right at our table. It was fun!

On the walk back to the hotel we passed a busy hospital. I saw a long line of people waiting in the open doorway. Aunt Heather said doctors in China don't have offices like they do in North America. People visit doctors at hospitals or clinics.

Near the hospital we stopped at a herbal pharmacy. The pharmacy looked like big drugstores at home, but it sold Chinese medicines. Aunt Heather bought a tea made from plant roots for her sore throat. She said the tea worked better than the medicine she buys at home.

I know some Chinese medicines and treatments are popular in North America. My mother had acupuncture treatments to stop the pain in her elbow when she played golf. I think I should find out more about medicine and health care while we are in Chengdu.

I also want to visit a kindergarten and a school one day. My guide book said China has 350 million children under the age of 15. That's a lot of children in school! I'd like to find out what schools are like here and if students study the same subjects we do. Aunt Heather asked our guide to arrange a visit for us to the school near the hotel.

I also want to find out more about the Chinese language. Aunt Heather has been teaching me a little Mandarin, which is China's official language. So far I've learned a few greetings and phrases. Chinese writing looks quite different from our alphabet. I hope I can learn more about it when I'm visiting the school.

I'm going to bed early tonight. I am still tired from the long plane trips and the travel in West China. I also need to be up early tomorrow. Aunt Heather hired a car, a driver, and a guide to take us out to the countryside tomorrow. She said nearly 70% of China's people live in the countryside. Tomorrow will be a chance for me to find out how people in rural areas live. Aunt Heather suggested I use her laptop to type my notes about the rural villages we will visit. I can have my photos developed and scan them in so it will look like a real magazine article!

I would like to go to a market in a village too. We have seen street markets in Beijing and in West China. It would be interesting to compare them with a market in the countryside in South China.

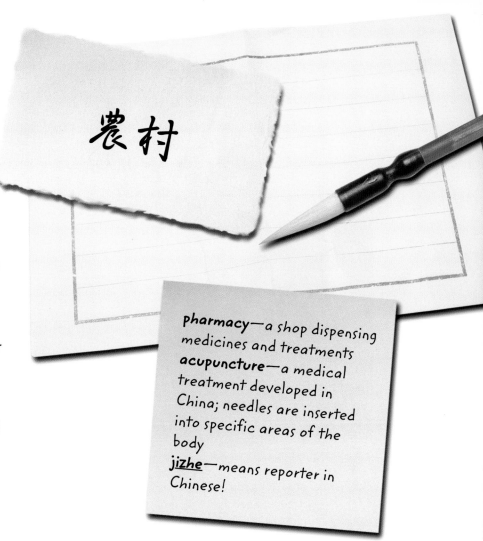

農村

pharmacy—a shop dispensing medicines and treatments
acupuncture—a medical treatment developed in China; needles are inserted into specific areas of the body
jizhe—means reporter in Chinese!

It's going to be a busy week. I have a long list of things I want to research. Aunt Heather said I am becoming a real jizhe. Working on my journal is a lot of fun, but I've discovered that being a reporter is tiring work.

I drew this in the market.

What I want to find out in Chengdu:
1. How does the geography of South China affect how people meet their needs?
2. What is life like in the countryside?
3. How is rice grown?
4. What is a Chinese market like?
5. What are schools like in China?
6. How is the Chinese language written?
7. How do Chinese people meet their needs for health care?

IMPRESSIONS

The countryside surrounding Chengdu is mainly green rice paddies, small towns, and villages.

4. The countryside in South China is one of China's main rice growing areas.

1. Every village house is surrounded by vegetable fields.

5. Market vendors use hand scales to weigh purchases.

2. I'd like to ride in one of Chengdu's bike rickshaws.

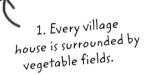

6. There are lots of well-off farmers near Chengdu who can afford to build new homes.

3. We saw logging trucks bringing trees to family-run sawmills.

7. People from the village often shop for small items at family run stands.

8. Some villages have paved roads but not all of them do.

11. Aunt Heather bought a sore throat tea at this Chinese pharmacy.

9. My Chinese is getting better. I can read this sign!

12. Some students were too shy to look when I took this photograph.

10. Chengdu is very crowded, with many apartment buildings.

GEOGRAPHY OF SOUTH CHINA

1 The heavy rainfalls produce lush green forests.

2 The Grand Canal is an important North–South link built in ancient times.

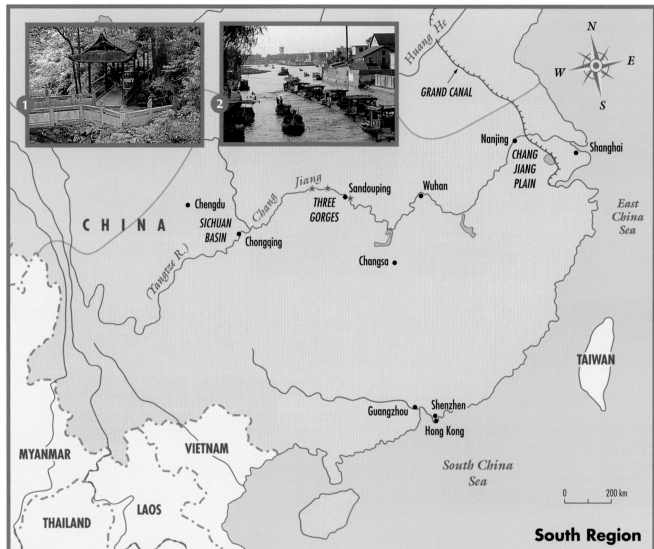

Landforms

- small area of plains
- 70% of region is mountains, hills, high plateau
- Sichuan Basin near Chengdu
- hillsides are terraced to grow rice and vegetable crops

Rivers

- Chang Jiang is China's longest river
- large number of rivers and lakes near Chang Jiang **delta**
- many **canals** join rivers and lakes
- Grand Canal connects South China to Beijing in North China

delta—a flat plain at the mouth of a river
canals—artificial waterways

- frequent flooding of Chang Jiang in rainy season; houses and farmland destroyed; large numbers of people killed

Climate

- hot, humid summers and cool winters (occasional frost; rarely snows); very warm all year in far south
- Chongqing, Wuhan, Nanjing, Changsa called "four ovens of China"; high summer temperatures (42°C)
- rainy season in summer; heavy rainfall, 750–2200 mm
- typhoons hit coastal areas between July and September
- flooding a common problem

Agriculture

- excellent farmland on plains and in Sichuan Basin; limited in mountains
- Chang Jiang Plain one of the oldest farmed areas in China
- main crops: rice, cotton, soybeans, grain, peanuts, beans, tea, tobacco, sugarcane, and tropical fruit (oranges, bananas, mangoes, lemons)
- often called China's "Rice Bowl": two crops of rice in summer, sometimes a third
- in mountainous areas, rice often grown, along with corn, wheat, sweet potatoes
- large pig farms
- silkworms raised for silk

Natural Resources

- many areas of excellent farmland
- hydroelectric potential
- forestry in mountainous areas; bamboo
- lakes suitable for fish farming; fishing in rivers, lakes, seas
- oil in South China Sea; oil and natural gas near Chengdu
- mineral resources (iron, copper, tin, lead, zinc)

Transportation

- large seaports along coast
- warm climate keeps ports from freezing; ships can dock all year
- ships carry goods into center of China on the Chang Jiang
- small boats and barges use many lakes, ponds, rivers, canals to transport goods
- railways, highways well developed
- many airports

Population

- very crowded
- most people still live in countryside
- many large cities; villages located close together
- Shanghai (12 million people) is one of the largest, most crowded cities in the world
- population almost all Han Chinese
- small number of minority nationality groups

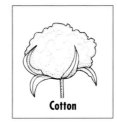

Rice

Cotton

Pig

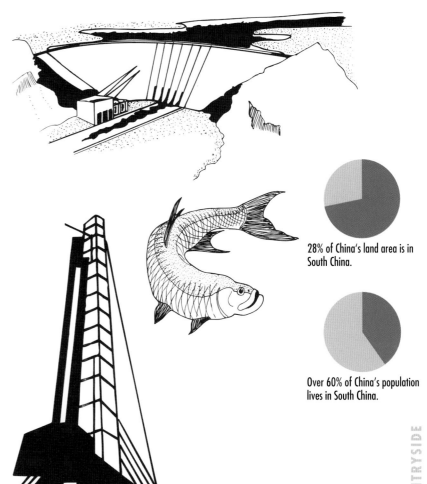

28% of China's land area is in South China.

Over 60% of China's population lives in South China.

TWO FISH POND VILLAGE

This was absolutely the best day of our trip! I learned so much about life in the countryside.

We left the hotel at 7 AM with our guide, Mr. Su, and a driver. Mr. Su is a university student studying English. He was born in a small town outside Chengdu so he knows a lot about life in the countryside.

Outside Chengdu the highways, shopping centers, and tall buildings quickly disappeared. The Chinese countryside seems to be green fields, small villages, and bumpy dirt roads. About every five minutes we passed another village. Aunt Heather told me that 70% of China's population lives in the countryside. That's a lot of people!

Unpaved country roads are usually bumpy and also very muddy in the rainy season.

The first exciting discovery was seeing water buffalo in a small pond. I really wanted photographs for my journal. Our driver parked along the edge of the gravel road and we walked along a narrow dirt path to the pond. The young boy looking after the water buffalo was very surprised to see us.

Water buffalo are quite different from North American buffalo. They have very wide, flat faces. Their long horns are bent backwards. The water buffalo in the pond looked quite funny with just their faces sticking out of the water. I thought they would be fierce, but they were very gentle animals. They let me get quite close.

Mr. Su told me that water buffalo need to soak their thick hides in water every day. This prevents their hides from cracking in the hot sun. Usually young children have the job of taking the family's water buffalo to a pond or river for a soak.

Families in the countryside are allowed to own their own animals. Water buffalo are used to plow fields and pull carts.

Rice paddies and corn fields surrounded the pond and crowded up the hillsides.

Rice paddies and vegetable fields completely filled the valleys and hillsides. Rice paddies are an incredible shade of green.

I could see several people working in the nearby fields. Some were hoeing and others were taking rice plants from their baskets and planting them in a muddy paddy field. They worked in muddy water up to their knees. Some of the workers looked as if they were my age.

Mr. Su told us that everyone in a family helps with farm work. He said that Chinese farmers still work in much the same way as farmers did hundreds of years ago. Hoeing, weeding, and planting in the rice paddies and vegetable fields are still done by hand. Farmers use very few pieces of farm machinery. Machinery is often too expensive for families to buy. A few farmers own small Chinese-built tractors. Water buffalo are also used to plow the fields.

New farming methods help farmers grow more kinds of vegetables than in the past.

I asked Mr. Su about the small stone boxes I could see on the hillside. He told me these were tombs. He said it was a traditional belief that the spirits of ancestors guarded the family home and village.

While we stood photographing the rice paddies, a young woman came up the dirt path. She carried a long pole on her shoulders with baskets attached to the ends. They swung back and forth as she walked. They must be very heavy when they are full.

It takes skill and practice to be able to balance such large baskets on a shoulder pole.

When she reached us on the path I tried saying hello in Chinese. It sounds like nee-how but is usually spelled *nihao*. She understood me, smiled, and replied. Mr. Su introduced us. The young woman was Zhang Lin. She said she lived in the village farther along the path.

Zhang Lin explained to Mr. Su that she was going home. She had spent the early morning in the family's vegetable fields weeding and picking some ripe vegetables. A member of her family would take these into the nearby market. She pointed out her brother loading baskets of vegetables onto bike carts and waved to another brother herding the water buffalo along the path.

Mr. Su explained to Zhang Lin that we were visitors from North America. We wanted to learn how people lived in the countryside. She smiled and pointed along the path. Mr. Su told us she was inviting us to meet her family in the village. We couldn't believe our good luck! We never expected to get an invitation to a village home.

We followed Zhang Lin along the narrow dirt path. Zhang Lin pointed out the family corn fields, rice paddies, and the squash and bean crops under a canopy of gleaming plastic. Zhang Lin told us her older brother went to farmer education classes two years ago to learn new planting methods.

Using plastic greenhouses allowed them to plant earlier and to grow more varieties of vegetables. Next year Zhang Lin's family hoped to grow peppers under the plastic canopy. She said that peppers were popular in the markets so they could sell them for a good price.

While we walked to the village, Zhang Lin explained to Mr. Su how her family earned money selling their crops. They sell most of their rice crop to the government. They sell their vegetables in the town market. Each morning Zhang Lin picks ripe beans and squash and loads them onto the family's two bicycles. With her brother's wife she bicycles 10 kilometers into the nearby town to sell the vegetables in the morning market.

As we got closer to the village we could see two small ponds gleaming in the early morning sun. Zhang Lin called out a greeting to the people gathered around the ponds. We could see they were dragging a net through the ponds. Zhang Lin explained that the village raised fish in the two ponds. The largest fish caught in the net would be put into buckets and sold in the town market. The money from the sale would be divided among the village families.

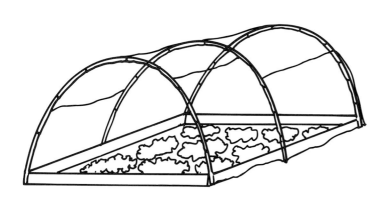

Several families work together to harvest the fish from the fish ponds.

While we watched, a woman in a small wooden tub checked the vegetation growing in the village fish pond.

Water from the field irrigation ditches keeps the fish ponds filled. Waste water from the village also flows into the fish ponds.

Zhang Lin told us the fish ponds were another way the village families made extra money. Many families in the village also operated small businesses. Zhang Lin's sister-in-law raises geese to sell in the market. Her mother sells bean curd and her father raises pigs. Zhang Lin's grandmother raises chickens and makes steamed buns to sell. Her two brothers work in the family fields and in the town-run lumber mill.

The family also owns two tractors. Besides plowing their own land, they plow fields for other families in the village. The tractors are also used to transport goods for other families into the town. It sounds like everyone in Zhang Lin's family works very hard!

The dirt path continued past the fish ponds up the hillside into the village. Aunt Heather pointed out to me that it was a traditional Chinese village with family homes arranged around narrow dirt lanes. Zhang Lin told Mr. Su that 65 people live here and all of them are related to her!

When we walked into the village people came out of their homes. Almost immediately we were surrounded by a crowd. People were very friendly. The children smiled at us and pointed to our cameras. They wanted us to take their picture.

There were lots of children in the village, more than I'd seen in the cities.

Traditional villages often contain fewer than a dozen homes. Others have 20 or 30 families. In smaller villages, everyone is related.

Zhang Lin took us down one of the dirt lanes to her home. Two small buildings were arranged around a pounded dirt courtyard. The buildings were made of dried bricks with tile and tin roofs. A shed for chickens stood in one corner along with a small building holding corn and rice being dried. Chickens scurried across the courtyard. The family toilet was behind the main building. The family had a well and an outside tap.

When we arrived, Zhang Lin's sister-in-law was washing dishes at the outside tap. Laundry and dishes were stacked beside plastic tubs near the well. Zhang Lin told us that the family washed dishes at the well, but did their laundry at the river.

Mr. Su explained that running water is not always available in villages. Homes may have a tap located outside the home. Wells are still common in the countryside.

Three generations of the family live together in Zhang Lin's family home. Zhang Lin introduced us to her sister-in-law, mother, and her grandmother. Zhang Lin told Mr. Su her grandmother was the oldest member of the family. She was respected by everyone in the village.

Zhang Lin explained that her grandmother was born in a village a few kilometers away. She came to this village when she was a bride of sixteen. She had made only an occasional trip into the town or to Chengdu. She's lived almost her entire life in sight of the green mountains surrounding the village.

While we looked around the courtyard, Zhang Lin's grandmother filled a pot from the outside water tap and carried it to a small fire. This burned in a brazier, which is a metal stand that holds lighted coals. She blew on the coals under the brazier to start the fire and make tea. As flames rose, she shoved in several corn stalks. Zhang Lin told us that most families in the village cooked with bottled gas or coal, but grandmother preferred the traditional way of using corn stalks.

Zhang Lin's brother looked after his daughter while his wife washed dishes at the outside tap.

Zhang Lin's family dry corn and rice stalks in a bin attached to their house. Her grandmother uses the corn stalks for fuel.

People in the village do most of their work outside the house. They cook and wash their dishes and clothes outside.

While Zhang Lin's grandmother made tea, her mother invited us inside the house.

The house had one large room for living and two small sleeping areas. The floor inside the house was concrete. The walls were plastered white. There was only one small curtained window. This made the room quite dark and cool. It would be pleasant inside the house during the hot summer.

Everywhere, wicker baskets, chests, and boxes were filled with ropes, tools, and bicycle parts. Food, cooking utensils, and bowls crowded onto a wooden shelf. A smaller second shelf held toothbrushes and toothpaste. The house did not have an indoor bathroom so the family kept their personal items here.

A nail hook held a variety of purses, bags, and a few tools. In one corner was a wooden frame with a plastic tarp draped over the top. It looked like a closet. Clothes were hanging on hooks attached to the wooden frame. Other clothes hung from hangers hooked into the frame. Suitcases and boxes were piled on a top shelf. I could see a small fan tucked away on a lower shelf in the closet.

The room had several wooden stools and chairs as well as a large red couch. Books, papers, and an ink bottle were spread out on the couch. Zhang Lin said her sister worked here to practice her school work. It reminded me of my bedroom when I do my homework. I think some of the family also slept in this room. Rolls of bedding and pillows were stacked in a corner.

Zhang Lin's village had electricity. The family had a single light inside the house and one electrical outlet. There were several extension cords to connect to appliances in the house. The family had a small black and white television. Zhang Lin told us the family hoped to buy a new color television later in the year if they had good crops.

Zhang Lin's family uses baskets, shelves, and hooks to organize their clothes, cooking utensils, and personal items.

The main room of the house contains a couch and a few smaller pieces of furniture. The children practice their school work on the couch.

After tea, Zhang Lin took us on a tour of the village. She showed us the small medical clinic and primary school. Both buildings were made of dried mud bricks with a tile roof.

Zhang Lin's village has a one room primary school and a first aid station. They got electricity a few years ago.

The clinic provided emergency first aid and treatments for minor illnesses. If a villager was seriously ill they had to travel to a hospital in the nearby town or Chengdu.

Zhang Lin asked Mr. Su if I went to school. He explained to me that like many girls in the village, Zhang Lin stopped attending school after Grade 4 to help work on the family's farm. The nearest high school was in town. Only a few boys were able to attend high school. Children in the village usually left school at the end of Grade 6.

After seeing the village, Zhang Lin's cousin took me out to his family's rice paddies to show me how rice is grown. I got some great photographs for my journal.

While I was looking at the rice paddies, Aunt Heather interviewed Zhang Lin's uncle. She wanted to find out how people in the village made a living.

Zhang Lin's uncle told Aunt Heather that in the past the families from several villages worked together on large government-owned farms called communes. The commune provided a job, food, and housing for everyone. All the land, farm machinery, and animals were owned by the commune. Farmers were not allowed to sell anything made at home or grown in household gardens. People were not allowed to work for themselves and make money for their families.

He said that now China had a new system called the responsibility system. Each family in the countryside is now expected to work hard and look after itself.

Farming families are allowed to contract land owned by the village or the town. This means they make an agreement with the village or town to farm the land. Farmers can decide what to plant and where to sell their crops. Farming families can own tractors, farm machinery, trucks, and farm animals. Zhang Lin's uncle said members of his family were very happy to be able to work hard and make money to improve their lives.

When it was time to leave, I gave everyone in Zhang Lin's family a pin from my home town. I wanted them to remember our visit. They seemed very pleased with the pins. The whole family came to wave good-bye to us.

When we got back to the car I realized we forgot to ask Zhang Lin the name of her village. Mr. Su suggested I call it Water Buffalo Village, but I liked the name Two Fish Pond. I know I will always remember the morning we spent with Zhang Lin in Two Fish Pond Village.

This is Zhang Lin's uncle, aunt, and cousins. Everyone in the village is related to each other.

GROWING RICE

For over 800 years rice has been China's most important food crop.

水稻

1 Rice paddies are often plowed using a hand plow pulled by a water buffalo because most paddies are too small for large plows and tractors.

2 Seeds are scattered in the mud, then the paddies are flooded with about five centimeters of water.

3 The seedlings grow for about three weeks in this crowded paddy.

4 When the seedlings are about 20 cm tall, workers transplant them into a second paddy. They grow for several months in the flooded fields.

5 After the rice grows and ripens, the water is drained from the paddy.

6 The rice stalks are cut, tied in bundles, and left to dry in the sun for about a week. Once the rice bundles are completely dry, they are hit against the inside of boxes and barrels to knock off the rice kernels.

7 The kernels are collected and spread in the sun to dry completely.

8 South China produces about 75% of China's rice and about 25% of the rice in the world using this paddy method.

XIAO KANG VILLAGE

After we left Two Fish Pond Village Aunt Heather and I decided to see the town market where Zhang Lin's family sold their vegetables.

As we got closer to the town of Suining, the road improved. There were fewer ruts and potholes. There was also more traffic. A constant stream of trucks and buses roared along the road. The people pedaling bicycle carts loaded with hay, sacks, and baskets of vegetables were often forced to dodge the speeding trucks. Mr. Su said people were heading into Suining for the market.

This is a very beautiful farming region. Rice paddies and fields of corn and vegetables stretched away to the distant Green Mountains. Most of the fields were crisscrossed with irrigation ditches. Aunt Heather said all these ditches were dug by hand and they needed constant repair.

Bike carts are often so loaded with hay and sacks it is hard to see the person pedaling.

This area closer to town seemed very well-off. The houses were new brick buildings with television antennas on the roofs. We saw a few farmers using tractors to plow the fields instead of water buffalo. There were more plastic covered greenhouses than we'd seen before.

When we stopped to photograph the fields, a crowd of young children and adults quickly gathered around us. They were very curious. Aunt Heather said that tourists don't usually visit the countryside area. People in the countryside rarely see visitors from other countries.

Many villagers had not seen foreign tourists before. They were surprised we wanted to take photographs of their fields and homes.

Dirt paths connect the tile-roofed village homes with the rice paddies and vegetable fields.

Two women working on the irrigation ditches in a nearby field joined the crowd around us. Mr. Su approached the older woman and asked her permission for us to see her farm. Her name was Grandma Tan. She smiled and pointed to the house in the small village at the end of the dirt lane.

Their family home was larger than the homes we saw in Two Fish Pond Village. The house was two stories high and made of brick. There was also a large brick barn for storing hay, corn, and rice.

Houses in the well-off villages are larger than homes in the cities. Several generations often live in the family home.

Grandma Tan pointed to a group of men working on a new brick house nearby. She told Mr. Su her eldest son was building a house for himself and his two married sons.

New farm homes are usually built of bricks with tiled roofs. The bricks and tiles are often made in a business run by a family or village.

All construction work is done by hand. Bricks and cement are carried in wheelbarrows. Rubble is cleared away by hand.

New farm homes often have electricity, inside running water, and gas stoves.

Mr. Su asked the women about their family. Grandma Tan told him that her three married sons, their wives, and eight grandchildren lived together in the first house.

Everyone in the family worked and added to the family income. The family used this money to spend on their basic needs. One son worked on the farm and one had a job at a town factory. Another son owned two tractor carts and carried bricks and building materials for local farmers. All of her daughters-in-law helped on the farm and ran the family's chicken and pig businesses. Two grandsons operated a brick-making business. Another grandson worked at a shoe-making factory in town.

Grandma Tan explained that her son's new house had inside running water and a new gas stove. They hoped to buy a new color television next year. Her daughter-in-law told Mr. Su she was looking forward to a washing machine. Her husband hoped to purchase a VCR soon. Their two sons bought motor scooters last year with the money they made from the brick business.

I said to Aunt Heather later that I noticed that people in the countryside did more than grow crops and raise animals. She explained that there are so many people in the countryside it is difficult for everyone to make enough money by farming. People have to find other jobs. She said more and more people in the countryside are working at factories and starting small businesses.

I've learned so much about life in the countryside, I'll need to add more pages in my journal!

MARKETS

Markets are busy centers in villages, towns, and cities throughout China. Village markets are usually held every morning. City and town markets operate all day. Some vendors have permanent stalls set up on the street. Some cities and towns also hold regular night markets.

" Farming families earn extra money by selling their crops in the markets. My family produces cucumbers, onions, tomatoes, and radishes to sell. We try to grow vegetables that are popular and sell for a high price. "

" We sell part of our rice crop to the government at a set price. We sell the rest of our crop at the market. The more rice we grow, the more we can sell at the markets. "

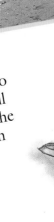

MARK CHEZ

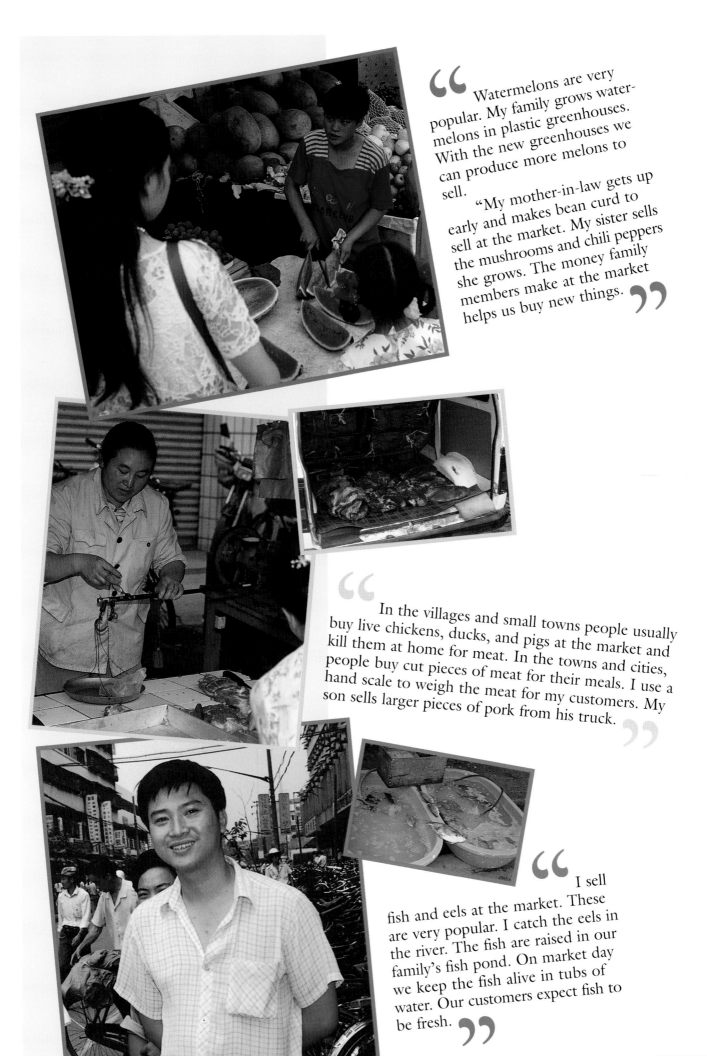

" Watermelons are very popular. My family grows watermelons in plastic greenhouses. With the new greenhouses we can produce more melons to sell.

"My mother-in-law gets up early and makes bean curd to sell at the market. My sister sells the mushrooms and chili peppers she grows. The money family members make at the market helps us buy new things. "

" In the villages and small towns people usually buy live chickens, ducks, and pigs at the market and kill them at home for meat. In the towns and cities, people buy cut pieces of meat for their meals. I use a hand scale to weigh the meat for my customers. My son sells larger pieces of pork from his truck. "

" I sell fish and eels at the market. These are very popular. I catch the eels in the river. The fish are raised in our family's fish pond. On market day we keep the fish alive in tubs of water. Our customers expect fish to be fresh. "

" My sister-in-law and I have a market stall selling clothing. We buy the shirts, pants, and shoes from the factories and sell them at the market. Prices in the market are lower than prices in the new shops and department stores. People like to shop here, so we make a good living. "

" I operate a bike repair stand with my brother. There are no jobs for us on the family farm. This is one way for us to make money for our families. "

" My family has run a small market stall selling household goods for the last year. In the past, individuals were not allowed to operate a business. Now the government encourages us to find new ways to make money for ourselves. "We buy the pots from the town factory and sell them in the market. People like to look at the new goods in the department stores but most things are too expensive for people to buy. People shop in the markets where the prices are lower. "

"Now that many families are earning more money, people can afford to visit a beauty salon to have their hair cut and styled. Young people especially want the latest styles. We operate our hairdressing business on the sidewalk in front of our family's small store. People often stop to watch us style someone's hair. We think we have started a good business for China today. In a few years we may be able to afford to open a beauty salon in the neighborhood and make a good living for ourselves."

"Going to the market is part of my daily routine. Sometimes I buy fresh soybean curd, porridge, or fried buns for my family's breakfast. After work I stop at the market to buy fresh noodles, meat, and vegetables for our evening meal. We don't have a refrigerator yet so I buy only what we need for the meal. In the market I can **bargain** for goods. In the department stores, customers must pay the set price."

"I make a good living selling noodles and deep fried buns in the market. My stall is famous for the good tasting buns."

bargain—discuss a selling price

THE MORNING MARKET

It was just getting light along the main road to town. Xu Hu and his brother stopped to adjust their load of vegetables, rice, and chickens. Everything was loaded into large wicker baskets hanging on their motorbikes.

The road was busy with farmers heading into town for the market. The closer they got to town, the more bike carts and wooden carts pulled by farm tractors filled the streets. Some bike carts loaded with fruit and vegetables were too heavy to pedal. They had to be pushed through the crowded streets. People riding to their jobs in factories and offices in town swerved around the slow moving vehicles.

Xu Hu and his brother had to push their motorscooters through the crowds once they were near the market. They passed several wooden carts loaded with pigs. They also saw some farmers with empty baskets returning to the country-side. Some farmers had arrived at dawn and sold out quickly to the early morning shoppers.

Xu Hu spotted his cousin Zhang Ce and her grandmother chatting on a street corner. Zhang Ce's family lived in a town apartment. She worked in a dress shop and wore the latest fashions. Grandmother Zhang preferred to wear the blue jacket and pants popular when Mao Zedong was leader of China.

People in town enjoyed shopping for new clothes and shoes in the market stalls and at the many clothing stores in town. Zhang Ce's dress shop sold the most popular new styles of dresses and skirts.

Zhang Ce walked with Xu Hu and his brother to her dress shop near the market and chatted about plans for a family wedding party next month.

Vendors near the market entrance had set up bright plastic tarps and umbrellas to protect their goods from the sun. There were vendors wherever there was space. Vegetables, fruit, clothing, and other goods spilled across the narrow street. Carts and bicycles filled every space. Many goods were displayed on low benches and tables set out in the street.

Most shops near the market were closed, with the metal doors pulled down over the entrances. Xu Hu and his brother parked their motorscooters near Zhang Ce's dress shop. While his brother unpacked their baskets of vegetables, rice, and chickens at their market stall Xu Hu helped Zhang Ce push up the dress shop's metal door. He helped Zhang Ce move the display racks and plastic models out onto the sidewalk.

All the clothes for Zhang Ce's shop came from factories in Shenzhen where they made the most modern and popular styles. A number of shoppers on their way to the market stopped to look through the shop's display. Xu Hu knew his sisters would like to own these beautiful clothes.

Xu Hu left his brother to watch their stall while he went to buy breakfast. Xu Hu liked coming to town. He enjoyed the day away from farm work and he loved the sights of the town. There were always exciting things to look at in the shops and interesting things to do. He passed a man who was writing a notice for a customer.

The new beauty shop was already filling with customers. The smell of perfumed shampoos floated out into the street.

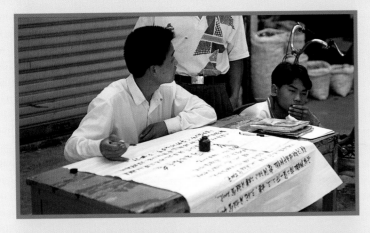

A young woman in the next stall was anxiously waiting for customers to buy the new supply of air conditioners she had for sale.

A crowd had gathered in front of the newspaper office to read a copy of the local newspaper.

Loud music blasted into the street from the shop selling music cassettes. This was one of Xu Hu's favorite shops to visit after the market finished. He also wanted to buy a new notebook for his youngest sister at the bookshop.

. At the pancake stall, Xu Hu bought breakfast for himself and his brother. The town was filled with many street stalls selling rice, dumplings, and noodles, but these delicious stuffed pancakes were his favorite.

On the way back to the market, Xu Hu stopped at the meat market for a few minutes to talk to his uncle. Next month his father would likely bring several of his pigs here. If he got a good price for the pigs the family might be able to get the new color television they had been saving to buy.

His uncle told him to stop by the building site a few blocks away where two of his cousins worked. The building site often needed workers to haul bricks and cement. Xu Hu's uncle suggested he try for a job there. His uncle said the **wages** were good.

Hurrying back to the market, Xu Hu thought about working in town. There was a shortage of jobs in the countryside. Not everyone could earn a living. Several people in his family already worked in town factories or businesses. Xu Hu smiled as he thought of living in town with his uncle. The money would help his family buy the new color television set and build the new house. Best of all, he could visit the stores more often.

wages—salary

AT SCHOOL

China has 350 million children under 15 years of age. Providing education for them is a very difficult and expensive task. To develop modern industries and farming methods China needs educated workers.[1] The Chinese government is encouraging students to complete nine years of school. The government plans to train a million new teachers and build thousands of new schools. They hope this will allow more students to finish nine years of education.

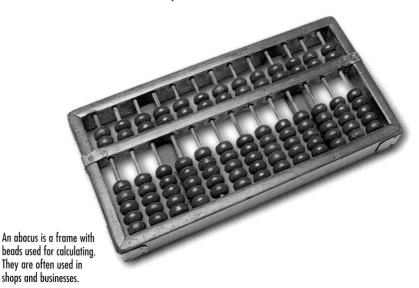

An abacus is a frame with beads used for calculating. They are often used in shops and businesses.

Yi Lin
(Primary school student in Chengdu)

"We start primary school when we are six years old. Primary school goes up to Grade 6. I go to school five days a week. Exercise class for the whole school starts at 7:30. Classes start at 8:30. I have classes all morning and then a two hour lunch break. After lunch I have classes until 4:30.

"My class studies mathematics and Mandarin (**Phutonghua**). This is China's national language. Next year we'll start learning English. We also study nature, history, geography, drawing, music, and physical education. We also have classes that teach us to be good Chinese **citizens**. We are taught to obey our parents, teachers, and the Chinese government.

"After school finishes, students are expected to clean their classrooms and keep the school yard tidy. Everyone in my school has a job to do."

Zhang Ming
(Pre-school teacher in Chengdu)

"In the cities young children attend nursery schools because both parents work. In the countryside, young children are more often looked after by older family members. Children attend nursery school until they are three. Children older than three attend kindergartens where they learn singing, dancing, games, and getting along with others."

---

[1] 22% of China's adult population cannot read or write.

Phutonghua—native dialect of Northern China and Beijing
citizens—inhabitants of a country

Chen Yuhua
(Primary school student in a village)

"This is my last year in primary school. In the cities most students finish primary school and attend a middle school. In the countryside many children leave primary school to work. I am lucky to have the opportunity to go to school. My two older brothers left primary school to work in Chengdu and my sister left to help with the farm work.

"Next year I hope to go to the **technical school** in town to study farming. I want to learn new ways for my family to improve our farm land.

"In the countryside most middle schools and technical schools are in the towns. It is difficult for village children to attend after they finish primary school."

Liu Hua
(Junior middle school student in small town outside Chengdu)

"I am in Grade 7 in junior middle school. Junior middle school goes from Grade 7 to 9. Senior middle school goes from Grade 10 to 12.

"There are 45 students in my class. We study Phutonghua, English, science, history, and mathematics. Mathematics is my favorite subject. We study how to add, subtract, divide, and multiply using an **abacus**. The abacus is an ancient Chinese hand-operated calculator. Sometimes using the abacus can be faster than using a pocket calculator!

"I wish my school had computers. Some middle schools in the large cities have computer labs for students.

"I do several hours of homework every night. Doing well in school is very important to my family. I must study very hard."

Wang Bing
(Senior middle school student in Chengdu)

"Last month I wrote the examinations to get into university. The examinations took three days. I studied long hours for weeks before the exams. My parents were very worried about how well I would do. They came to the school with me when I wrote the exams. They waited outside the school gates with the other parents. I hope to get high enough marks to be accepted at university. A university education will help me get a good job so I can look after my parents."

---

technical school—school where skills for trades such as electrician, welder are taught

RIGHT: Calligraphy is considered an art form in China.

BELOW: The two characters for *xie xie,* Mandarin for "Thank you," are identical.

BELOW: The Mandarin word for "Hello" is *nihao.*

LANGUAGE

Speaking Chinese

Over one billion people speak Chinese. It is one of the most widely spoken languages in the world.[1]

There are a number of Chinese **dialects**, or forms of the language. Each one has different vocabulary and pronunciation.

Seventy percent of the people in China speak the Mandarin dialect. In 1949 the government decided to use Mandarin (Phutonghua) as the national language. Having a common language helps people meet their need for **communication**. A common language also builds feelings of unity in such a large country. Children are required to study Mandarin in school. Television, radio, and many Chinese movies use the national language.

The Cantonese dialect (Guangdonghua) is also widely spoken. People in Hong Kong and the region near the city of Guangzhou (Canton) speak Cantonese. It is also spoken most often by Chinese people living in North America.

Tones

Spoken Chinese uses tones of voice as part of the meaning of words. The word *ma,* for example, can mean "mother," "house," or "scold." The meaning depends on the tone of voice. The four tones are level, rising, dipping, and downward. In English we use a rising tone at the end of questions, such as "Did she go?" Saying "So?" when we are annoyed, uses a dipping tone. Saying "No!" firmly uses a downward tone.

Writing Chinese

All Chinese dialects use the same writing system. Chinese is written using line pictures called **characters**. Characters are picture-like symbols that stand for an object or idea.

The art of writing characters with a special brush and ink is called **calligraphy**. It takes many years of practice to learn to write Chinese well.

[1]English is another one of the most widely spoken languages.
communication—the giving or exchange of information

Characters

Chinese characters were developed in ancient times. People drew signs and symbols on wood, bone, silk, pottery, or bamboo strips. This system of writing influenced other Asian languages. Chinese characters are still used in Japanese, which is also written using characters. Part of the Korean language is based on Chinese.

Chinese characters are not sounded out like alphabet letters. Students must learn to recognize each character and what it represents. Most characters contain a meaning, and some hint about the sound. Words are often made up of two or more characters. These combinations must be learned as well as the individual characters. To read a newspaper one needs to know more than 2000 characters. A well-educated person can recognize more than 8000 characters.

Traditionally, Chinese has been written in columns from left to right on a page. Today Chinese is more often written across the page left to right. The characters on this page are written in a column and on the next written across the page.

Pinyin

Pinyin is a method of writing Chinese using the **Roman alphabet**. The Roman alphabet is the 26 letters used to write English and most of the European languages. In China, Pinyin is sometimes used along with Chinese characters on signs.

Some initial sounds are pronounced differently in Pinyin than in English. This list should help you pronounce the Chinese names in this book.

c	<u>ts</u> as in ba<u>ts</u>
q	<u>ch</u> as in <u>ch</u>ild
r	<u>zhr</u> as in mea<u>s</u>ure
x	<u>sh</u> as in <u>sh</u>ape
z	<u>dz</u> as in lor<u>ds</u>
zh	<u>dg</u> as in lo<u>dge</u>

Other initial sounds are much the same as in English. See the pronunciation list on page 152 for some more examples.

Chinese Characters and Computers

Modern personal computers can easily handle the thousands of Chinese characters. The keyboard, however, is a problem. Keyboards are designed for languages that use small alphabets of letters or symbols. It is difficult to design a keyboard that will type thousands of characters. One method used in China is to type the words using Pinyin. The computer changes the typed Pinyin into characters to display on the screen. China and Japan have spent billions of dollars researching the problem of how to type characters. This conflict between traditional Chinese writing and new technology has not yet been completely solved.

The Four Blessings

Long Life	Wealth
長壽	發財

Luck	Happiness
好運	快樂

HEALTH CARE

Since 1949 the health of Chinese people has improved. People can now expect to live longer, healthier lives.[1]

Today there are many health care and medical services in cities. There are fewer medical services in the countryside. Over 80% of the doctors and hospitals are in large cities and towns, and expensive equipment is only available in city hospitals. Rural villages usually have only a small medical clinic. Village clinics are staffed by people who have taken a two year training course. Seriously ill people must travel to a hospital if they need an operation or special treatment.

In the cities, medical expenses are usually paid for by a worker's company or work unit. In the countryside, most people pay for treatments themselves. Operations and treatments for serious illnesses are often too expensive for them to afford.

The majority of Chinese people live in the countryside. The government wants all people to have health care and medical services. More hospitals in towns and more village clinics are being built. Medical workers for clinics are being more highly trained.

Traditional Chinese Medicine

Traditional Chinese medicine includes acupuncture and herbal medicines. Large hospitals in cities have clinics that offer both **Western medicine** and traditional medicine. Clinics in the countryside usually use traditional medicine.

Acupuncture

Thousands of years ago Chinese doctors discovered that some areas of the body were sensitive when a person was ill.

Acupuncture treatments involve inserting needles into the body at special points. The patient feels only a small sting like a mosquito sting.

When the sensitive areas are pierced with needles, the pain or the illness often disappears. Doctors have recorded hundreds of these special points on the human body.

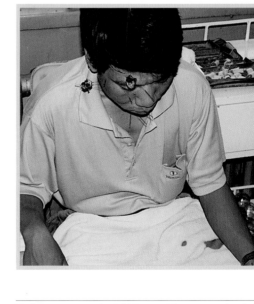

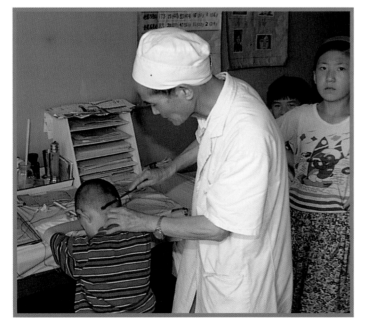

---

[1]Life expectancy in 1949 was 35 years; today it is 70 years.
Western medicine—mainly uses surgery, manufactured drugs, and specialized medical equipment to treat illnesses

Herbal Medicine

Herbal medicine uses dried plant roots, leaves, stems, and flowers, **fungi**, minerals, bones, and other animal parts. Many of these materials contain **chemicals** similar to those in pills commonly used in North America.

World Connections

Acupuncture and herbal medicines are popular in many countries. Foreign doctors go to China to learn more about these treatments for illness. Acupuncture has an amazing ability to stop pain. Doctors are interested in using it to treat sports injuries and **arthritis**. Western doctors are also interested in some herbal treatments, such as those used to treat severe burns.

North America is an important producer of **ginseng**. North American grown ginseng is sold to China and other Asian countries for use in herbal medicines.

Many people in the world worry about the effect Chinese medicine has on the world's wildlife. Certain horns, paws, bones, and fins are used to make popular herbal medicines. Each year millions of animals around the world are killed and body parts sent to China. Many of the animals hunted are **endangered** species.

ABOVE: A dried seahorse
TOP RIGHT: Ginseng root
MIDDLE RIGHT: A Chinese pharmacy

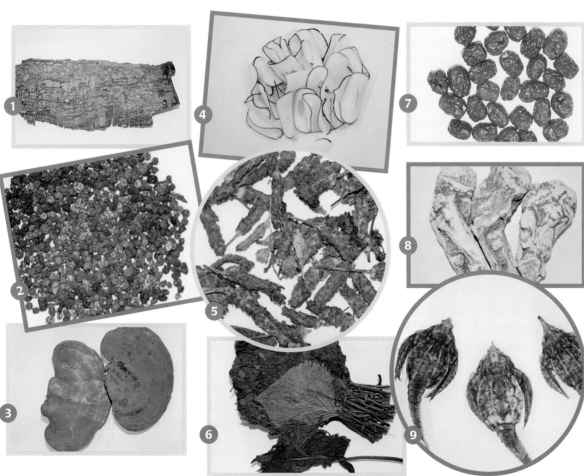

1 Eucommia bark
2 Schisandra seeds
3 Ling Zhi mushroom
4 African sea coconut
5 Selfheal spike leaves
6 Perilla leaves
7 Red dates
8 Dang Quei root
9 Flying fish

fungi—mushrooms, toadstools, molds
chemicals—basic substances that may be combined to make other substances
arthritis—a disease causing swelling and pain in joints

ginseng—a plant with a thick, forked root, used in tonics
endangered—threatened with extinction

LOOKING BACK
Activities

Impressions (pages 54–55)

1. a) **Look** carefully at the photographs on pages 54–55. **Classify** them into the three types of needs.

   b) **Write** a paragraph **explaining** what these photographs tell you about how life in China is changing.

Geography of South China (pages 56–57)

1. On a world map **compare** the latitude positions of Chengdu, Chongqing, Shanghai, Guangzhou, and Hong Kong with places in North America. **List** similarities and differences of climate and seasons you would expect to find, based on latitude position.

2. ➡ On pages 30 and 50 you started an on-going project on the geography of China. Use information from pages 56–57, the mini-atlas at the back of the book, and your atlas to add the following to the South China region:
   a) **Mark** or **glue** on it:
   - Chang Jiang, Huang He, Chang Jiang Plain, Grand Canal, East China Sea, South China Sea, Taiwan, Vietnam, Myanmar, Thailand, Laos, Shanghai, Chengdu, Shenzhen, Hong Kong, Chongqing, Guangzhou, plus 10 other cities
   - areas where the following are grown or located: rice, tea, cotton, soybeans, pigs, bamboo, hydroelectric power, oil, natural gas, iron, copper, tin, lead, zinc
   b) **Draw** people to represent the population of South China on your pictorial graph of the population of China. Place them near your representations of the populations of North and West China for comparison.

3. **List** examples of how the geography of South China affects how people meet their basic needs.

Two Fish Pond Village (pages 58–64)

1. Imagine you are with Taylor in the Chinese countryside. **Write** a letter home describing your visit to Two Fish Pond Village. Include details of how people make a living and general living conditions.

2. **Construct** a model, a mural, or a diorama depicting life in Two Fish Pond Village.

3. In small groups, develop a **role-play** in which students take the roles of Taylor and family members in Two Fish Pond Village. Role-play should include information about how people make a living and the way of life in the countryside.

Growing Rice (page 65)

1. **Make** a poster illustrating how rice is grown.

Xiao Kang Village (pages 66–67)

1. After you have finished reading Taylor's journal of her visit to Xiao Kang Village, **write** your own captions for Taylor's photographs. Captions should include information about life in the countryside.

2. **List** ways family members in a village make a living.

Markets (pages 68–75)

1. **Make** a market diorama or mural depicting the market described on pages 68–71, or the town depicted in the narrative The Morning Market on pages 72–75.

At School (pages 76–77)

1. Use a Venn Diagram to **compare** schools in China with schools where you live. Venn Diagrams are explained on page 146.

Language (pages 78–79)

1. Develop a short Chinese language lesson for your class. Prepare charts and practice activities to help students learn to speak a few words of Chinese.

2. Writing Chinese characters with special brushes and ink is called calligraphy. **Practice** the art of calligraphy using the four blessings as your subject. **Display** your work.

Health Care (pages 80–81)

1. Imagine you are a writer for a North American health magazine. **Write** a short article on traditional Chinese medicine. Include information on benefits and possible negative consequences.

Chapter Review

1. Use one of the strategies on page 142 for **recording** the following vocabulary: terrace, humid, markets, responsibility system, communication, herbal medicine, acupuncture, endangered. Put this assignment in the WordBook section of your China binder.

2. **Create** and **present** a word poster with one of the chapter's vocabulary terms. Word posters are described in the Appendix on page 144.

3. **Classify** the photographs in this chapter into
   • physical, psychological, and group needs
   • physical, psychological, and group wants

4. **Check** the organization of your activities for this chapter in your binder:
   • chapter title page, notes, activities, maps, and illustrations in Activities section
   • definitions in WordBook section

   • China Journal writings
   • Tools of Learning notes

5. Do either a) or b).
   a) **Summarize** your research notes for this chapter into a retrieval chart. Either make your own chart (see page 144 in the Appendix) or ask your teacher for a summary chart for this chapter.
   b) **Answer** Taylor's questions on page 53.

6. When you have finished reading about Taylor's visit to the countryside, **write** your own captions for the photographs on pages 54–55. Do not write in the textbook. Include information from what you learned in the chapter.

7. **Create** a set of postcards, an illustrated poem, or a story about the Chinese countryside or some experience you had there. Include three facts and three impressions or personal feelings.

8. **Create** a game, puzzle, skit, radio show, song, or rap about Chengdu. Include at least 10 facts in it about life in the Chinese countryside.

9. **Create** a travel brochure, magazine or newspaper article, pamphlet, or display encouraging North Americans to visit China's countryside.

10. In question 1 on page 31 under Government you started a **web** showing how the Chinese government influences or controls the way the people live. Add information from this chapter to your web.

Moving to the City

Shanghai

Our next stop in South China is Shanghai. We flew here this morning. Shanghai is even hotter than Chengdu. Luckily the taxi from the airport was air conditioned and so is our hotel room. We are staying at a brand new hotel.

My guide book says that cities in China are growing very fast. More and more farm land is being taken up for housing, office towers, highways, and airports each year. From the hotel room all I can see are new buildings and dozens of construction cranes at new building sites.

After we unpacked, we took the subway to downtown Shanghai. Everywhere there were crowds of people. Aunt Heather says that Shanghai is one of the largest cities in China. Each year hundreds of thousands of people move here, making it even more crowded. People move from the countryside because there are more jobs in the cities and city jobs pay more money. People also like the shopping and entertainment that cities provide.

There is certainly lots of shopping here. We spent the day looking through all the new department stores and shops on Nanjing Road, the main shopping street in Shanghai. It was so crowded in front of the cosmetic counters of one department store that I couldn't move.

I was very surprised that Shanghai department stores look exactly like the stores at home. Aunt Heather says that Chinese people today are buying more clothing, furniture, and other goods for their homes because they earn more money than they did in the past. My class will be surprised to see how similar a Chinese shopping center is to the ones at home.

Now we are in Shanghai I am looking forward to seeing Xu Min. She has been living with Aunt Heather while she goes to university and she is home for the holidays. Tomorrow we will visit her family. I hope her family will let me take photographs of their apartment. I want to show my class what it is like living in a Chinese city. I hope Xu Min will also be able to help me find out more about Chinese families and marriage.

I also want to find out about how China is trying to control its population. My library book said China had a huge population that was growing rapidly. The government has been using a plan called the One-Child Family Plan to reduce the rate of growth. Xu Min is an only child. Maybe she can tell me more about this plan. Xu Min also promised to take me on a tour of her neighborhood.

One day this week we're taking a boat cruise down the Huangpu River which runs through the city. Shanghai is a very important trade center. Ships from all over the world come here to unload goods or to pick up Chinese products. Shanghai is one of China's most important port cities.

We will also be meeting several of Aunt Heather's friends who work for Shanghai newspapers. I hope I can ask them about the ways Chinese people make a living.

There are so many things to do and see here—I think we need longer than a week!

进城

What I want to find out in Shanghai:
1. What is it like living in a city apartment?
2. What are families like in China?
3. What is a neighborhood like?
4. In what ways do Chinese people earn a living?
5. What do Chinese people like to buy?
6. How is China trying to control its population?
7. Why are more people moving to the cities?

port—harbor; where goods are loaded onto and off of ships
construction—building
cosmetic—product to beautify the face

IMPRESSIONS

Shanghai is an incredible mix of old and new buildings. There are new high-rise buildings everywhere but still lots of older neighborhoods and gardens. This must be one of China's largest and busiest cities. There are people everywhere!

4. Shanghai is one of the busiest seaports in the world.

1. Some of the older buildings in Shanghai were built by the British.

5. The moon gates in the garden of this older style Chinese home are beautiful.

2. Shanghai is one of China's most modern cities.

6. Most families we saw in Shanghai had only one child.

3. Many families live in small apartment buildings. Some still have only outdoor running water.

7. Nanjing Road is the main shopping street in Shanghai.

8. Selling goods from bike carts is one way people make money.

12. Families that earn more money are spending more on appliances for their homes.

13. People in Shanghai like to shop for modern styles of clothing.

9. Shanghai has many new shops and department stores.

10. Only very well-off families can afford to buy a computer for their home.

14. A new department store and office tower is being built across from our hotel.

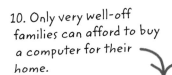

11. Shanghai has a population of over 12 million. I think everyone owns a bicycle!

HOMES

Most people in the cities live in apartments. Chinese apartments are larger than they were in the past, but still small. Most apartments contain one or two rooms used for sleeping, a bathroom, and a small kitchen area.

Inside a Chinese Home

Balcony		
Bedroom and living area	Entrance and hallway	Bathroom
Kitchen and eating area		Bedroom and living area

.5cm=1m

Bedrooms and living space are often combined in small Chinese apartments.

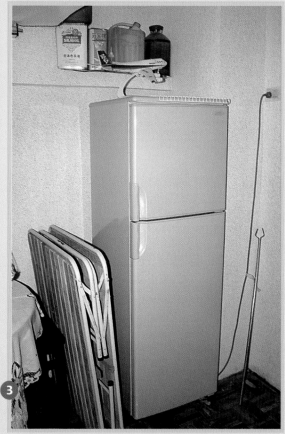

❶ Space inside apartments is limited. People in China have traditionally used their balconies as extra living space. Apartments usually don't have closets. Clothing and personal items are piled on shelves or stored in dressers, cupboards, trunks, and boxes. Families use rooms for several purposes, such as sleeping, watching television, working, and eating.

❷ Traditionally, cooking is done using a coal or charcoal fueled burner. Some families use a two-burner gas hot plate. Kitchens do not usually have ovens.

❸ Many Chinese families can now afford **electrical appliances**. With so many people using more electrical appliances there are often shortages of electricity. Refrigerators are now common in city apartments. Apartments are small, so sometimes the refrigerator is stored in the living or sleeping area.

electrical appliances—toasters, mixers, frying pans, coffee pots, and other small machines that run on electricity.

家居

4 Many apartments have an electric water heater to heat water. Not all city homes have inside running water. Homes in older areas may have outside taps and sinks.

5 Newer apartments have bathrooms with tubs and showers. It has been a tradition that families share public toilets provided for each street.

6 In many older city neighborhoods public toilets are provided for residents. In recent years, cities have replaced older toilets with new modern facilities.

7 Many families now own washing machines. Dryers, however, are not common. Most of China is hot for much of the year. This allows people to dry clothes on bamboo poles outside their windows or on balconies.

8 Eating areas in most apartments are very small.

9 Bedrooms in Chinese homes are similar to those in North American homes. Apartments are usually small so bedrooms are also used as living areas.

10 Families may have a Buddhist **shrine** or a shrine for the family ancestors.

11 Space is limited in city apartments and there are usually no closets. Clothing is hung on racks or stored in trunks and cupboards.

12 In the warm summer months, people often take advantage of the "free" city electricity. They visit, read, eat, watch television, or play cards on the sidewalks under the city street lights. In hot weather people even sleep on cots outside on the sidewalk where it is cooler.

shrine—a place where religious articles are kept

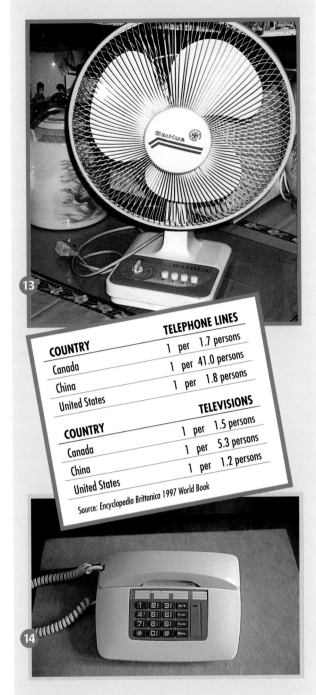

COUNTRY	TELEPHONE LINES		
Canada	1	per	1.7 persons
China	1	per	41.0 persons
United States	1	per	1.8 persons
COUNTRY	TELEVISIONS		
Canada	1	per	1.5 persons
China	1	per	5.3 persons
United States	1	per	1.2 persons

Source: Encyclopedia Brittanica 1997 World Book

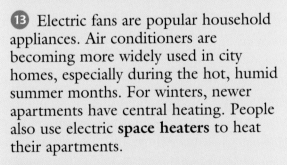

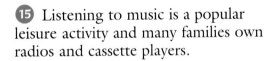

13 Electric fans are popular household appliances. Air conditioners are becoming more widely used in city homes, especially during the hot, humid summer months. For winters, newer apartments have central heating. People also use electric **space heaters** to heat their apartments.

14 Home telephone service is not widely available in China. There is also a long wait to have a phone installed. Sometimes older apartment buildings have one phone which is shared by all the families in the building.

15 Listening to music is a popular leisure activity and many families own radios and cassette players.

16 Many families in China own televisions. A few families own CD players. VCRs and video compact disk players are common in many Chinese homes.

17 Only very well-off families have computers at home. Very few are connected to the **internet**. CD-ROM players are not common.

space heaters—electrical appliances providing heat to rooms; often used in place of a central furnace
internet—a network linking computers around the world

A CHINESE FAMILY

The family and family **responsibilities** are very important in Chinese life. Until recently most people lived in large **extended families**. An extended family is usually made up of three or more generations. Grandparents, parents, and children lived together in one house or apartment.

Recently family organization has changed. Many people today live in **nuclear families**. A nuclear family consists of a husband and wife, or a single parent, and children. Nuclear families are especially common today in the cities. Extended families are still common in the countryside.

Getting married and having a family is very important. In recent years the government has encouraged young people to delay getting married and to have only one child to help reduce the number of children born each year.

Interview with Xu Min's Family

Xu Min

"The family has traditionally been the center of Chinese life. Belonging to a family and keeping close connections with grandparents, uncles, aunts, and cousins is very important. Most people spend their lives thinking and living as a family rather than as individuals.

"We believe family members have a responsibility for one another. The family tries to support each other."

Xu Min's Mother

"Traditionally Chinese families have been large. Several generations lived together. When I was growing up it was common for grandparents, uncles, aunts, and cousins to live together in the family home. Today Chinese families are smaller."

Xu Min's Aunt

"By law, women in China have equal rights with men. In daily life, however, this is not always so. While women in the cities are as well educated as men and can work at their choice of jobs, women in the countryside often do not have as much schooling. There is very little variety in the kinds of work for women in the countryside. Jobs may be assigned by work units rather than chosen.

"Because there is a shortage of jobs in China, women are sometimes encouraged to give up their jobs and stay home. This makes more jobs available for men.

"Women in China have many responsibilities. After a full day working in the farm fields, office, or factory we also have responsibilities at home. We are expected to keep house, prepare meals, shop, and care for children and older family members."

responsibilities—duties

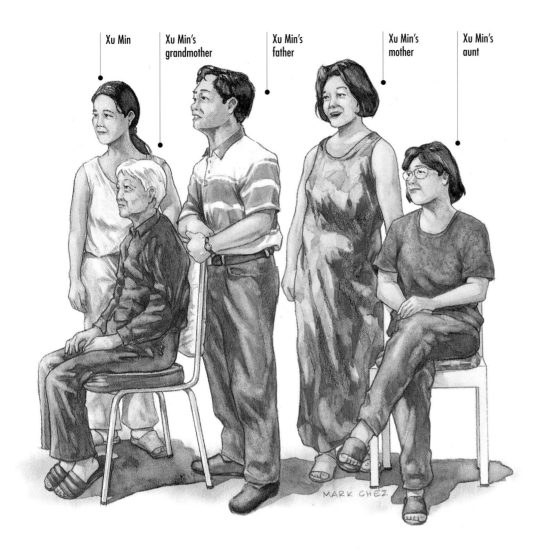

Xu Min   Xu Min's grandmother   Xu Min's father   Xu Min's mother   Xu Min's aunt

MARK CHEZ

Xu Min's Father

"A woman in China is expected to marry and provide a son for her family. Young women in China are not encouraged to remain single and make a life for themselves.

"Most young people choose their own marriage partners. Young men must be at least 22 and young women 20 to get married.

"In the countryside, weddings often involve the entire village and a large banquet. The bride and groom sometimes wear traditional wedding outfits. In the cities, couples often have a small wedding ceremony with the bride wearing a **Western** wedding dress and the groom wearing a suit and tie. Many new shops in the large cities now sell Western style wedding dresses and tuxedos.

"Chinese couples are allowed to divorce. In recent years the number of divorces has increased."

Xu Min's Grandmother

"In the past grandparents often helped look after the house, prepare meals, and take care of the young children. Today, grandparents do not always live with their families. Many older people live in retirement homes. Many still live with their families but they spend more time on leisure activities and hobbies."

Xu Min

"Many things about family life have changed in recent years, but traditional values have stayed the same. Family connections are very important. Older family members are respected. We help and support family members. Families are still an important part of Chinese life."

Western—refers to anything that is non-Chinese or non-Asian

A CHINESE NEIGHBORHOOD

People do most of their shopping in the neighborhood where they live.

❶ A typical neighborhood market is full of people and activity. Traditionally people in China shop daily for vegetables, meat, noodles, and fruit at small neighborhood shops and market stalls.

❷ People often stop for snacks or take-away food from street food stalls. Noodles, stuffed dumplings, and steamed buns are popular take-away foods.

❸ Most shops, restaurants, and services are operated by **residents** of the neighborhoods.

❹ Neighborhood shops and market stalls offer clothing, appliances, and repair services. People often have their hair cut at street barbershops.

❺ In many city neighborhoods, retired people often volunteer to look after the buildings where they live. They take out the garbage, sweep the streets each morning, and make sure that the public toilets are cleaned.

residents—people who live in a building or neighborhood

HUA NONG (FLOWER LANE)

In the early morning darkness Zhang Hui woke to the "swish, swish" of bamboo brooms sweeping the deserted street. Every morning several retired residents of Hua Nong swept the street clean. They also cleaned the street's public toilet. For Zhang Hui the sound had become her alarm clock, telling her that life was stirring again on Hua Nong.

From her bed Hui had a clear view of life in her neighborhood. The lane was one of the many tree-lined streets in an older neighborhood of the city. Her bed was next to the apartment window so that she could look out onto the street.

Hui had been born with a damaged spine. She had been in a wheelchair all her life. This had never stopped her from going to school and enjoying activities with her friends. She was only in bed because she had pneumonia. Hui's doctor had allowed her to come home from the hospital but she must rest in bed for another two weeks.

Hui had been home from the hospital for a week. By now she could recognize all the sounds of her lane. She could tell the time of day just by the footsteps and voices on the street outside her house.

After the sweepers' swishing brooms, Hui heard the older residents of the lane heading to their *taijiquan* exercises in the park. Then her neighbor Wang Po would walk by on his way to the park with his two cages of yellow finches singing noisily.

By six o'clock Hui could hear her parents hurrying about the home. They too went to the park for morning exercises. On the way home from the park Mother usually stopped at the stalls in the market. She bought deep-fried buns and fresh bean curd for their breakfast and noodles and vegetables for their evening meal.

By seven o'clock Hui heard the school children laughing and chatting as they headed down the lane. A few of her friends stopped for a quick chat with her about homework or last night's television show.

After eight Hui knew the lane would be quiet. Anyone still at home would be busy with household chores. The older residents sat on the shady sidewalk chatting with neighbors, playing cards, sewing, washing clothes, looking after the babies, or tending their flowerpot gardens. Occasionally a vendor made his way down the lane trying to sell his fruit, vegetables, or noodles to the residents.

Hui spent these quiet afternoons reading, doing her schoolwork, and daydreaming about when she would be allowed out of bed. For Hui, the best times in the neighborhood were the summer evenings. Everyone came out to the cool sidewalk to enjoy the evening breezes. The neighborhood was filled with people until the late evening. Meals were prepared and eaten under the trees. Babies slept in their strollers. Children and adults sat and chatted with their friends. People strolled along sidewalks, stopping at the stalls set up by the food vendors. Father always bought Hui ice cream or a popsicle from the street stall.

Hui could hardly wait to be well. "One more week," she thought. She smiled as she leaned back in bed and listened to the sounds of the neighborhood. "Only one more week!"

---

taijiquan—ancient Chinese exercises often called *tai chi*

EARNING MORE

Chinese people today are earning more money than in the past. Many can now afford to buy new appliances and furniture for their homes. Incomes for people living in the cities have increased in the last ten years. The majority of families in the cities are able to meet their needs for housing, food, and clothing. A very few people, such as sports stars, popular movie actors, popular singers, and very successful business owners, are millionaires. These people can afford to buy a house, a car, and the other items they want.

1 The Chinese government is encouraging people to "work hard for themselves and get rich." Workers may have a second job or operate a small business in addition to their work unit job. Some people earn extra money by operating stalls at street markets.

2 A few people have started their own businesses. They operate small restaurants, street food stalls, beauty parlors, barbershops, bicycle repair shops, bakeries, magazine stands, clothing shops, and furniture stores. Business owners pay a small tax to start their business but they may keep all the money they make.

3 Many people operate small snack and food stands set up on the sidewalk. Fried buns and dumplings are popular snacks prepared at these sidewalk stands.

4 Selling fish and seafood is another way people can make money. The fish are usually kept alive in buckets so customers can see how fresh they are. Shrimp is a popular seafood ingredient in Chinese cooking.

THE GOOD NEIGHBOR STAND

Liu Mei dishes the last batch of beef noodles into a bamboo container, wipes her hand across her damp forehead, and takes a deep breath. It is only nine in the morning, but Liu Mei has been working for nearly three hours. For the last hour she has been too busy chopping, stirring, or serving to even look up. Now, Liu Mei looks around her noodle stand with pride.

The Good Neighbor Stand is a concrete hut with a tin roof. Inside there are a few storage cupboards and two charcoal stoves near the front of the stall. A long bench runs down one side where Liu Mei and Chang Yun, her sister-in-law, prepare the vegetables and noodles. Underneath the bench are wicker baskets filled with vegetables. Above are found jars of spices for the soups.

For the breakfast rush Liu Mei usually moves the charcoal stoves and **woks** out onto the wide sidewalk. The morning customers line up with their baskets to collect the fresh noodles and porridge to take home. Some eat their noodles sitting at the two benches set out on the sidewalk.

The Good Neighbor Stand always has a long line of customers waiting for the tasty beef noodles and peanut porridge. In the afternoon they prepare a lunch box meal of rice, vegetables, and bits of meat.

Two years ago there was no Good Neighbor Stand. Liu Mei had a job at the government run factory, but the pay was low. She wanted to buy more things for her family. She and her sister-in-law discussed what kind of business they could operate and still keep their factory jobs. They remembered the long lines of people at the only noodle stand on their street. They decided there were enough customers for another noodle stand. They applied to the government to open the Good Neighbor Stand near the bicycle factory where Chang Yun worked.

The profits have been good. In the last two years Liu Mei and Chang Yun have made enough to buy color televisions, refrigerators, and washing machines for their apartments.

A few years ago Liu Mei would not have been allowed to start a business and make money for herself. In Mao's China people were not allowed to work for themselves. Workers were paid the same no matter how hard they worked. The government tried to provide the same pay, food, clothing, and housing for everyone. This was called the "**iron rice bowl**." The "iron rice bowl" provided everyone with their basic needs.

Allowing people to work for themselves and earn extra money is part of China's new responsibility system. People are encouraged to take responsibility for deciding how they will make a living. Now the Chinese government is encouraging individuals to start their own businesses and work for themselves.

Liu Mei and her sister-in-law work long hours at their business. When the clothing factory at the end of the street **laid off** workers, Liu Mei hired two women to help with the stand. The stand is exhausting work but Liu Mei and Chang Yun feel it is worth it so they can give their families a better life.

---

woks—Chinese cooking pots
iron rice bowl—a Chinese phrase meaning a person is guaranteed a job for life, and so will always eat
laid off—no longer employing someone

Earning a "Golden Rice Bowl"

Xu Min introduced us to her neighbors who were "earning a golden rice bowl."

Yao Lan

"In the past the Chinese government decided what jobs people would do. Now, many people want more than an 'iron rice bowl.' They want to earn more money and have a '**golden rice bowl**.' A 'golden rice bowl' is enough money to buy more than the basic needs of food and clothing."

Li Jianguo

"For nearly 30 years I worked as a machine repairer in a government factory. The company started losing money and laid off most of the workers. At first I was very upset. Workers at the factory had always been guaranteed a job and a place to live. I was worried about losing the company apartment, but the company allowed us to continue living in their apartments if we paid rent. It was hard to change, but after 30 years repairing the same machines this was a chance for me to do something I wanted. I borrowed money from my family to take a driver training course. Now I drive a taxi for a government taxi company. I usually work from 5 AM until 9 PM. I make more money than I did at the factory because I decide how long I work. My new job is great!"

Song Xuequn

"I worked for four years at a factory making shirts. Last year the factory laid off many of the workers because it was losing too much money. This allowed me to finally choose the type of work I wanted. I decided to open a small computer business in my neighborhood. I work very hard and spend long hours at my shop. I like working for myself but there are problems. Now I must sleep at the shop. When I worked at the shirt factory I could apply for a company apartment when I married. Now it will be hard for me to get an apartment when I marry."

Wu Heng

"When I came to the city I could not find a job. I worked for a few months hauling electric fans on my bicycle from the factory to shops. My cousin suggested we start a small bicycle repair business. We have a good location on a busy road and often repair 30 bicycles a day. We sleep right at our repair shop."

Zhou Shumei

"Last year my husband and I decided to start a business to earn extra money. Our daughter needs a computer for her high school work. To save the money we started a small flower business. Early in the morning before work at my regular job I buy the flowers at the flower market. My husband sells them in the evenings after work. We take turns selling flowers on our days off. People often buy flowers when they go to visit a friend or attend a wedding or birthday party. Business is good. We made a small **profit** this year. We hope to buy our daughter a computer soon."

Zhao Qizheng

"When I retired I needed a job to help my family. I bought a bike cart and started a small newspaper and magazine business near the bus station. Most days I work from 5 AM until 8 PM. Sometimes a family member helps. The profits are small, but I have enough money to buy small things for the apartment and new toys and clothes for my grandson."

Hu Zemin

"My wife and I work at the same factory. Our pay depends on how well the company does. If the company makes money, we are paid more. If the company loses money, we get less pay. To make more money, we operate a stall at the night market selling material and clothing supplies. We usually make more money at the market than we do at the factory. The money from the market stall helps us buy new things for our apartment."

profit—money made after expenses

SPENDING MORE

Chinese families have more money to spend on basic needs. Many families have money to spend on **luxury** goods for themselves and their homes.

1 Today there are more things to buy than in the past and more places to shop.

2 Chinese people shop at expensive new department stores and shopping centers, small neighborhood shops, and stalls in street markets.

3 Street markets provide many kinds of new and used goods, food stalls, and personal services at lower prices than usually found in the department stores.

4 Most shoppers pay for items with cash. Even very expensive items are usually paid for in cash. Checking accounts, credit cards, and automatic teller machines are just becoming available in cities.

5 Family members often combine their money to purchase expensive items for their homes. Many luxury items such as refrigerators, big screen color televisions, washing machines, and air conditioners take months of saving.

luxury—things wanted that are beyond basic needs

花費增多

6 Chinese shoppers are spending more money on clothing. Women wear brightly colored dresses, skirts, blouses, and high-heeled sandals. They have their hair styled in beauty salons. Cosmetics are now widely available.

7 Shirts, slacks, and Western style suits are worn by men. Sunglasses, baseball caps, jeans, T-shirts and running shoes are very popular with younger people.

8 Foreign brands of running shoes, such as Nike, Adidas, and Reebok, are especially popular.

9 In some places, scooters and motor-cycles are popular purchases. People are also replacing their plain black bicycles, common throughout China, with brightly colored bicycles and mountain bikes.

10 Cars are too expensive for most families. Only very well-off people can afford to purchase them. Many vehicles are owned by companies or government departments. Chinese factories today produce a variety of cars and trucks. Some vehicles are imported from Pacific Rim countries.

11 Household electrical appliances are popular items with shoppers. About six million Chinese-made air conditioners are sold each year in China. Small shops also sell used washing machines and television sets.

12 People have more spending money. Video game stores are becoming popular. Ice cream and soft drink stands are common throughout the cities.

13 China is one of the world's leading producers of computers. Home computers are not common, but many people have computers at work.

14 In recent years, cellular phones have become extremely popular because there is no delay for installation. Several million cell phones are in use in China today.

15 Stores selling tapes and CDs are becoming more common in the cities. More people also own cameras. They are taking more photographs and more shops sell cameras and develop film.

16 Many families can afford to eat out occasionally at a restaurant or street stall. Fast food restaurants are especially popular with younger Chinese.

DEPARTMENT STORE SHOPPING

As the crowds streamed through the doors of the department store, Ming smoothed the jacket of her blue store uniform and began her speech: "Please try our new Golden Dragon eye shadow." Ming held out the sample case of blue and green eye shadow. She swiftly applied a thin smooth film of frosty green to the customer's eyelids.

Crowds of shoppers gathered around Ming and the other cosmetic sales clerks. Everyone was interested in the free samples and anxious to try the new brand. Perfumes, face creams, and makeup have been recent additions to Chinese life. In the past cosmetics were not available. Chinese women did not wear makeup, curl their hair, visit beauty shops, or wear Western style clothes. In 1979, the year Ming was born, China began a new program of **opening to the world**. Since then there have been many changes. Now, everyone wants to wear the latest styles. They spend as much money as they can afford on stylish clothes and shoes.

The crowds of shoppers surging into the department store were very fashionably dressed. Ming admired the bright yellow chiffon dress and curly hair of the young woman waiting in front of her. Ming keeps her hair long, but Ming's mother and aunt regularly visit a beauty salon to have their hair cut and styled. Ming's grandmother also has her hair done fashionably. Grandmother told Ming that since everyone was changing, she must too.

When Ming's mother and aunt were her age everyone wore the same blue jackets and pants with plastic sandals. There were few things to buy in the stores and few luxuries in people's homes.

Now, with everyone in the family working and contributing, Ming's family has money to buy several new items for their home each year. In the last two years her family has purchased a new color television, a new refrigerator with a freezer section, a washing machine, and two more electric fans for their apartment.

As the crowds of shoppers swirled past Ming, her mind drifted toward the evening. After work she will meet her friend, Xiulan. They will go to a new fast food restaurant and then to see a movie. They might even have time to walk through the night market to look at the displays of dresses and shoes. With pleasant thoughts of the evening ahead, Ming smiled at another customer and offered her a sample of Golden Dragon eye shadow.

---

opening to the world—a government plan to allow exchange of goods, ideas, and people between China and other countries

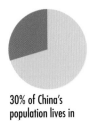

POPULATION

China has a population of approximately 1.3 billion people. This is nearly one quarter of the world's population. China has more people than any other country in the world.

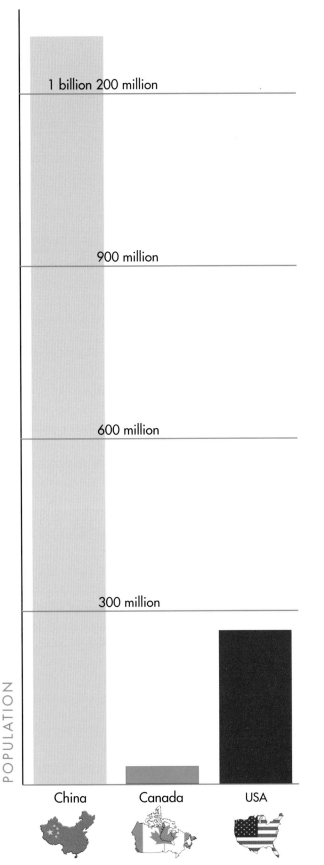

Population Compared to Canada and the United States[1]

Source: *UN Statistics 1997*

1 billion 200 million

900 million

600 million

300 million

POPULATION

China Canada USA

[1]This population graph shows the number of people in China in 1997. Elsewhere in the textbook the figure estimated for year 2000 is used.

30% of China's population lives in urban areas

Population Growth

The population of China increases by 15–20 million people each year. This yearly increase is as large as the total population of many countries in the world.

Effects of Population Growth

Population growth has affected China's environment and how the people meet their needs. It also has impacts on the rest of the world.

As China's population grows larger, more food, water, **energy**, minerals, and other materials are needed to meet their needs. Natural resources are **depleted**. Forests are cut down to provide wood for building and fuel for cooking. Dams on rivers provide hydroelectric power and river water for farms. Drinking water supplies are used up. **Sewage** and garbage produced by the large population pollutes land resources. Automobiles and factories produce air pollution.

As the population increases more of the farm land is used for non-farming purposes. New apartments, offices, shopping centers, airports, and highways are built on farm land. Each year there is less farm land to grow food and more people to feed.

To feed its large population China must **import** grains such as wheat and rice from Canada, the United States, and other countries. Feeding more than one billion people is a major problem.

It is expensive for the Chinese government to provide housing, health care, and education for such a large population.

Providing work for so many people is also difficult. China has the largest number of workers in the world, but millions are still without work.

China's huge population could affect world natural resources. For example, if everyone in China ate more fish the world's fish resources could quickly be depleted. If everyone in China ate bread instead of rice, vast amounts of grain would have to be imported to make bread for the Chinese population. This would create grain shortages elsewhere.

Controlling Population Growth

The Chinese government wants the population to be no larger than 1.4 billion at the year 2010. To slow down population growth the Chinese government introduced the "one-child family plan." This plan encourages couples to have only one child. Controlling population growth is not popular because China has a tradition of large families. Many people do not like being told to have only one child. The government has tried to convince people that it is important for their country and for the world that China control its population growth.

MIDDLE RIGHT: Cities are expanding into farming land.
BOTTOM RIGHT: A one-child family in the city

---

population growth—the amount the population of a place increases or decreases
energy—power, force; e.g., electrical energy
depleted—exhausted, reduced
sewage—waste from humans and animals
import—bring into the country

China has 25% of the world's population.

China has only 7% of the earth's farmland.

One-Child Family Plan Today

Aunt Heather: "Thank you for meeting with us today, Yang Mo. North Americans have heard about China's 'one-child family plan.' Could you tell us why China introduced this plan?"

Yang Mo: "I work at the university keeping track of China's population growth. Even with the one-child family plan, China's population grows by almost 17 million people a year. It is important that China control population growth. We have 25% of the world's population but only 7% of the farmland on earth. We are concerned that we will not be able to provide food for our growing population."

Aunt Heather: "Describe the one-child family plan for us, please."

Yang Mo: "Couples who have only one child receive more pay at work, better housing, free health care, and a place for their child at daycare, kindergarten, and school. One-child families are also allowed to buy a better quality of rice and meat.

"Couples having more than one child wait longer for housing and a school placement. Health care is not free. Families can also be fined for having more than one child."

Aunt Heather: "In your opinion has the one-child family plan been successful?"

Yang Mo: "It has been a difficult task to control China's population growth. The one-child family plan has not been completely successful. China has a tradition of large families. Families want several sons because sons are expected to look after older family members. Families in the countryside want several sons to help with the farm work or the family business.

"The plan has been more successful in the cities. Most couples in the cities choose to have only one child. City couples feel they can provide a better life if they have only one child. The small size of city apartments also encourages couples in the cities to follow the one-child family plan."

Aunt Heather: "My research indicates that recently the Chinese government has allowed some families to have more than one child. Which families are allowed more children?"

Yang Mo: "Families in the countryside are still encouraged to have small families, but they are allowed to have a second child if the first is a girl. People from minority nationalities are also allowed to have more than one child."

SETTLEMENT PATTERNS

China's population is not spread evenly throughout the country. Some areas are very crowded with people. Other areas have few people.

Most of China's population lives on the plains along the eastern coast of China. Very few people live in the high mountain areas in West China or in the dry desert areas in northwest China.

China has at least 40 cities with populations over one million. Some cities such as Shanghai have over 12 million residents.

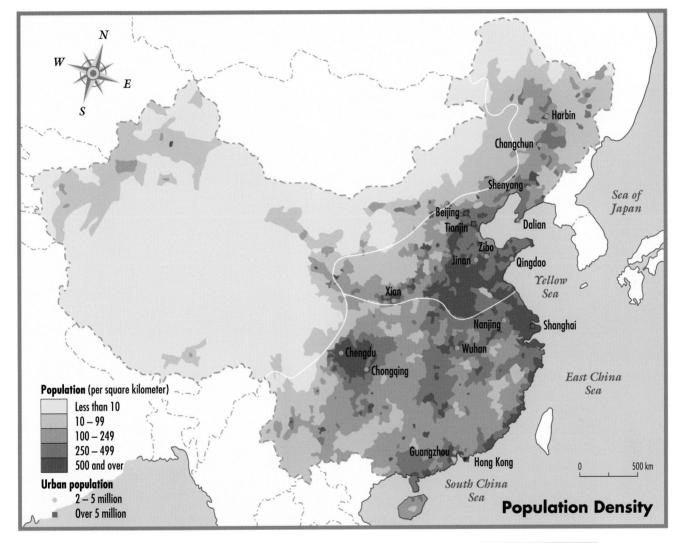

Population (per square kilometer)

- Less than 10
- 10 – 99
- 100 – 249
- 250 – 499
- 500 and over

Urban population

- 2 – 5 million
- Over 5 million

Population Density

ABOVE: The population density map shows the number of people in a square kilometer. The white lines divide China into the three geographic regions used in this book.

BOTTOM: New apartment buildings in a crowded coastal city

Movement to Cities

Traditionally most of China's population has lived in the countryside. In the last few years, millions of people have moved from the countryside into the cities. Nearly 30% of the population now lives in cities. At any time, there are also approximately 100 million people who are traveling from city to city looking for work. In the coming years, even more people will likely move into the cities.

Train stations in large cities are often crowded with people from the countryside who come to the cities looking for work. In rural areas, many people cannot find work. The cities offer people a chance for a job that pays more money than they could make in the countryside. Wages in the city can be three times higher than those in rural areas.

People come to the cities hoping to find jobs. Factories, building projects, and road construction projects hire many workers. Sometimes entire villages are hired for construction projects. Workers move to the city for a short period of time and live in temporary housing on the construction site. Living conditions can be poor.

LOOKING FOR A BETTER LIFE

The Shanghai train station and the nearby streets were filled with people sitting on bundles, sacks, and suitcases. Some slept on the steps of the stores. They had all come from villages and towns in the countryside to find work in Shanghai.

Ke Jun and his cousin had come to Shanghai eight days ago from their village 500 kilometers away. They had been sleeping at the train station, taking turns searching for work, and talking to the other young men searching for work. The train station and the nearby streets were filled with groups of people from the countryside waiting with their bundles.

Ke Jun had been working in various places for five years. He had hoped to attend high school after finishing all the grades offered at his village school. Instead he started looking for work. His family needed the money Ke Jun could earn working.

Ke Jun's first job was in a nearby town working at a building construction site. He worked ten hours a day carrying heavy buckets of sand, cement, and bricks on a bamboo pole. It was exhausting work. The buckets were heavy and difficult to balance. He and the other workers slept in a tarp-covered shelter on the building site. The pay, however, was more than he could have made working on the farm. He sent most of his pay back to his family in the village.

When that job finished Ke Jun started moving from town to town looking for more work. He usually worked carrying materials and supplies at construction sites.

Sometimes he found a job on a road building crew digging trenches or carrying loads of gravel on his bamboo pole.

Ke Jun and his cousin were hopeful they would find good jobs in Shanghai. Each day one of them stayed behind at the train station to look after their bundles while the other one searched for work.

As he waited for long hours in the crowded railway station Ke Jun felt sad and lonely. He missed the family meals and conversation with his grandparents, uncles, and cousins.

He missed the quiet darkness of the nights on the farm. Shanghai was bright all night because of the flashing electric signs and street lights. The traffic was constant and noisy. Just crossing the busy four lane streets could be a dangerous and frightening experience.

As much as he missed his family and home Ke Jun knew that he would not stay in his village. If he found a job in the city, the money he sent home would help all of his family. In the city there was a chance to make a better life for himself and his family. But first he needed a job. Ke Jun searched the faces of the crowds streaming into the station. He desperately hoped he would see his cousin returning with good news.

LOOKING BACK

Activities

Impressions (pages 86–87)

1. Look carefully at the photographs on pages 86–87 and classify them into the three types of needs.

Geography (pages 56–57)

1. Write five statements explaining how the geography of South China affects people in Shanghai. Consider housing, clothing, transportation, food crops, sports.

Homes (pages 88–91)

1. Using information from pages 88–91, make a list of the new technology that is available in city homes. Write five statements explaining how technology may affect a family's way of life.

2. Imagine you are with Taylor visiting a family home in Shanghai. Write a letter describing the home.

A Chinese Family (pages 92–93)

1. Create a chart or poster illustrating ways families in China have changed in recent years and ways they have stayed the same.

A Chinese Neighborhood (pages 94–95)

1. In small groups, develop a role-play in which students take the roles of members of Xu Min's family. The role-play should include information about Chinese family organization, how families are changing, traditional family values, and activities in a typical Chinese neighborhood.

Earning More (pages 96–99)

1. Create a poster illustrating ways people earn a living in Chinese cities.

2. In complete sentences explain the following Chinese expressions:
   • work hard for oneself and get rich
   • an iron rice bowl
   • a golden rice bowl
   • responsibility system

3. Write a short paragraph explaining how ways of earning a living are changing in China.

4. a) Use a chart to compare ways people make a living in Chinese cities and ways of making a living where you live. Charts are explained on pages 144–146.
   b) Evaluate the information. Are there similarities? Are there differences?

5. List some advantages and disadvantages of starting a small business instead of working for the government or a government-run factory.

Spending More (pages 100–103)

1. Refer to Making Charts and Graphic Organizers in the Appendix on pages 144–146. Use a Venn Diagram to compare items Chinese families would like to purchase with purchases your family would like to make.

2. Using the information on pages 96–103, classify items into Iron Rice Bowl basic needs and Golden Rice Bowl wants.

3. Write a paragraph on how trade might affect what items Chinese families can buy with their increasing incomes.

4. Create a poster illustrating how shopping and spending money has changed in recent years in China.

Population (pages 104–106)

1. CHALLENGE: The front endsheet of this text is a pictorial graph. Create a different graph or chart using the same information.

2. Find a way to **illustrate** China's rural and urban populations **using graphs, charts,** or **models.**

3. **Create** a poster or chart illustrating the possible effects of China's population on China's environment, the world's environment, and how the Chinese people meet their needs.

Settlement Patterns (pages 107–109)

1. **Write** a short paragraph explaining why people from the countryside are moving to the cities.

2. a) Working with a partner, make a **list** of problems that could affect cities if more people from the countryside came to live in the cities. Consider how cities would provide basic needs for populations of more than 10 million.
   b) Provide **suggestions** that might be useful in solving urban problems in China based on your knowledge of North American cities.

Chapter Review

1. Use one of the strategies on page 142 for **recording** or adding information to the following vocabulary: iron rice bowl, golden rice bowl, luxury goods, responsibility system, opening to the world. Put this assignment in the WordBook section of your China binder.

2. **Create** and **present** a word poster with one of the chapter's vocabulary terms. Word posters are described in the Appendix on page 144.

3. Use a comparison chart to **compare** earning a living in a large Chinese city with earning a living in the countryside. You may wish to **review** your notes on In the Countryside in the Activity section of your China binder. Comparison charts are explained on page 146.

4. **Classify** the photographs in this chapter into
   • physical, psychological, and group needs
   • physical, psychological, and group wants

5. **Check** the organization of your activities for this chapter in your binder:
   • chapter title page, notes, activities, maps, and illustrations in Activities section
   • definitions in WordBook section
   • China Journal writings
   • Tools of Learning notes

6. Do either a) or b).
   a) **Summarize** your research notes for this chapter into a retrieval chart. Either make your own chart or ask your teacher for a summary chart for this chapter.
   b) **Answer** Taylor's questions on page 85.

7. When you have finished reading about Taylor's visit to Shanghai, **write** your own captions for the photographs on pages 86–87. Do not write in the textbook. Include information you learned in the chapter.

8. **Create** a game about Earning More—Spending More in China. Include at least 10 facts in it.

9. In question 1 on page 31 under Government you started a **web** showing how the Chinese government influences or controls the way the people live. Add information from this chapter to your web.

The New China

Shenzhen

Hong Kong

It seems like just a few days ago that I was organizing my journal on the flight to China. Now we have only a few days left in Shenzhen and Hong Kong, and my journal is nearly full! I found so many things to write about in China. It really is an amazing place!

I've never seen so many new buildings as here in Shenzhen! When Aunt Heather visited China the first time this area was mostly farmland. Now, Shenzhen is a city of three million people, with thousands of factories. Our guide said that Shenzhen is a Special Economic Zone. These are areas along the coast where the Chinese government has encouraged new factories and industries to develop.

Aunt Heather said I will be even more dazzled by the development in Hong Kong. Hong Kong was controlled by the British until 1997 but it's now a part of China. She says the shopping centers and department stores in Hong Kong are terrific. They sell goods from all around the world. Aunt Heather said the Chinese government is using Hong Kong as a model for Shenzhen's development. The government wants the rest of China to become as developed as Shenzhen and Hong Kong.

The Chinese and foreign-owned factories in Shenzhen make many items sold in North American stores. This is one reason North American

trade with China increases each year. Aunt Heather told me that nearly half of the toys sold in North America are made in Chinese factories. My running shoes and T-shirt were both made in this country.

If the Chinese government wants to develop other areas of China they will need new sources of electricity. In some of the places we visited, there were a few hours during the day when there was no electricity. The Chinese government is building new hydroelectric dams because of the shortage of electricity. When Aunt Heather was in China last year she saw the new Three Gorges hydroelectric dam being built across the Chang Jiang. When it's finished it will be the largest hydroelectric dam in the world. She printed some information about the dam from her computer for me to put in my journal.

Before we take the express train to Hong Kong I want to get photographs of Shenzhen's new trains, highways, and airports. Transportation here is quite different from what we saw in the countryside.

Another surprise here is the huge number of cellular phones we've seen. I even saw people riding bicycles and talking on their cell phones.

We're going to spend our last day in China touring Hong Kong. I was hoping we could see the dragon boat festival and races, but they are held in June. I bought a Chinese calendar showing all the traditional festivals and new holidays. There is even a festival celebrating Chinese young people. It would be fun to spend a whole year in China and see all the festivals.

On our last night in Hong Kong we're going to eat at a special restaurant to celebrate the end of our trip. Before I came here I didn't know there were so many styles of Chinese cooking. Many of

the Chinese people in North America come from South China and cook Cantonese style food. That's the style usually served in North American Chinese restaurants. I really liked the spicy Sichuan food we had in Chengdu and the steamed dumplings they make in North China. My class will be surprised I also ate pizza and fried chicken at Western style fast food restaurants.

These last few days will be busy. I want to get my last rolls of film developed and finish my journal. I also want to buy a few more souvenirs and presents to take home to my family and friends. There's lots to do before we leave!

新中國

development—creating changes for a purpose
Three Gorges—a narrow river channel on the Chang Jiang flowing through an area of steep cliffs
Hong Kong means "fragrant harbor" in Chinese
foreign—from outside China

What I want to find out in Shenzhen and Hong Kong:
1. How have new technologies affected how the Chinese meet their communication and transportation needs?
2. Why is there more development in the Chinese cities along the coast?
3. How is the Three Gorges Dam affecting the way people live?
4. How is China using its resources?
5. What is China doing to protect the environment?
6. How have Chinese eating habits changed in recent years?
7. What do people in China do for fun?
8. What holidays are celebrated in China?

IMPRESSIONS

Shenzhen

Everything is new in Shenzhen. There are new office towers, factories, department stores, restaurants, and highways. Less than 20 years ago Shenzhen was a small fishing village surrounded by farmland. It had far fewer people and little development.

3. This model of a traditional family home is built around a small courtyard.

1. Shenzhen has some of the tallest towers I have ever seen.

4. There are many new department stores and shopping malls.

2. This model shows the traditional Chinese style used in building pagodas.

5. Shenzhen has very modern transportation.

6. Many companies have built new office towers in Shenzhen.

10. Most of the clothes sold here are made in Shenzhen factories.

7. Not all the workers can afford to live in expensive apartments.

11. As Shenzhen gets bigger, more farmland disappears.

8. The traditional shoulder pole is still common.

9. Huge shopping centers are replacing small street markets.

12. Sometimes workers from the countryside live in shelters they build from scrap building materials.

Hong Kong

Hong Kong is even more crowded and developed than Shenzhen. It's hard to move on the crowded sidewalks. The streets are constantly filled with traffic. Even the harbor is crowded with ships and ferries. Every street seems to have a new building project. I've never seen so many restaurants or places to shop.

5. There is constant construction here.

1. Lots of buildings were built by the British when they controlled Hong Kong.

6. The Star Ferry is the most common way to get across the harbor.

7. The streets in Hong Kong are often a jungle of neon signs.

2. Hong Kong's many millionaires can afford sailboats for fun.

3. The curved tile roofs of traditional Chinese buildings are distinctive.

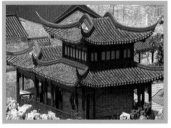

4. Fantastic view of Victoria Harbor and the huge office buildings!

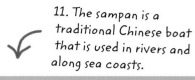

11. The sampan is a traditional Chinese boat that is used in rivers and along sea coasts.

8. The street markets are very, very crowded.

12. Most of the main streets are at least four lanes wide.

9. This crowded city is even built on land created by filling in part of the harbor.

13. Many residents of Hong Kong follow the Buddhist religion.

10. Land is so expensive most buildings are built as tall as possible.

COMMUNICATIONS

Communication means to exchange information. Good communication systems help people feel they are part of one country. Having a sense of belonging is a social (or group) need and so is communication. Good communication systems help the government explain new laws and plans to everyone in the country. Communications help businesses buy and sell goods. In a country as large as China, exchanging information with everyone is difficult. People in China communicate in both traditional and modern ways.

Taylor: How are information walls like this used?
Aunt Heather: This is a good way to make information available to a large number of people. Newspaper articles and government announcements are posted on the walls of buildings. Anyone can read them and post comments about them.

Taylor: How else is information communicated to so many people?
Aunt Heather: China's 800 radio stations provide news and entertainment programs. There are more than 2000 newspapers and 7000 magazines providing local and national news. Foreign news stories, however, must be approved by the government before they can be printed or broadcast.

Taylor: How does the Chinese government play a role in communications?
Aunt Heather: Television, telephones, fax machines, satellites, and the internet are new ways information and ideas are exchanged. The government wants Chinese businesses to be successful. They also want to control the flow of information and ideas into China. For example, foreign news agencies must have their stories checked by the Chinese government. All internet users must register with the government. Home satellite dishes are **banned**, so people cannot watch foreign television shows. Government owned or approved satellite dishes, however, are an important use of new technology for communication.

Taylor: China will need lots of new technology to meet their changing communication needs.
Aunt Heather: North American, European, and Asian companies already sell satellite, telephone, and fax equipment here. This is another trade connection between China and North America.

banned—not allowed

Changing Communications

Lu Ming

"New technology has changed how information is communicated. Television is now the most important **news medium**. China has more than 600 television stations and over 850 million television viewers. Television programs let people find out what is happening in other parts of China and the world. The government, however, carefully selects what foreign television programs are shown."

Liu Guohua

"Computers have also changed how people communicate. The number of personal computers in homes is small, but many people use computers at work. A few **cybercafes** have also opened in large cities. At a cybercafe, customers pay a small fee to use a computer and the internet. Over a million computers are sold here each year. China could become the world's largest computer-using country."

Chen Lianghua

"Businesses need to be connected to the world by phone, fax, and computer. There are not enough phones in China. Providing phone service to so many people is a problem. Installing new phone lines across a large country with so many mountains is a difficult job. That is why more people are using wireless cellular phones. There is a long waiting time for phones to be installed, so cellular phones are popular. China will likely have over 18 million people using cellular phones by the year 2000.

"Phone service needs to improve in the countryside. The number of '**telephone villages**' is increasing, but many small villages still do not have telephones."

news medium—the way news is communicated (the plural of medium is media)
telephone villages—villages where over 60% of the homes have a private telephone

TRANSPORTATION

People in China use traditional and modern methods to meet transportation needs.

1 In the city, walking is still a very common way of getting around. In some rural areas, it is the only available transportation. Animals and human power are used to pull carts or to transport goods short distances. Tractors and trucks are slowly replacing carts pulled by animals.

2 In Hong Kong, buses are a common sight on the crowded, narrow streets. Large cities such as Shanghai, Beijing, and Guangzhou have new subway lines to transport people. Companies from Europe, North America, and Asia supply the equipment to build these new subways.

3 Most roads were single-lane and unpaved in the past. Today, modern multi-lane highways connect cities. Highway construction is done by hand as well as with modern road-building equipment.

4 The use of boats on rivers, lakes, and canals is a traditional means of transport in China. This sailing ship is called a junk. Junks were used for many centuries to carry people and goods down the broad rivers and across seas. Thousands of barges, boats, ferries, and ships still use China's river highways every day.

交通工具

5 Railways are important to China's transportation system. The Beijing–Hong Kong railway line, is a new north–south connection. More railway services are needed to handle the increasing demand for passenger and **freight** transportation.

6 China has built modern container seaports along the coast. Railway lines deliver **containers** packed with goods to the seaports. They are loaded directly onto ocean-going ships and transported to countries around the world.

freight—transportation of goods in containers
containers—large, box-like metal receptacles used to transport goods on ships and railway cars

7 Rivers, lakes, and canals provide important connections between places. Coastal freighters carry goods north and south. Ocean-going ships and coastal freighters are an important link in the transportation system. China's 160 seaports are always crowded with ocean-going ships from around the world.

8 The demand for air transportation is constantly increasing. By the year 2000 China will be among the world's top users of air transportation. North American and European jet manufacturers sell airplanes to China's airlines and train Chinese pilots.

DEVELOPMENT

Development means creating change for a purpose. This often involves an increase in industries and services in a place. As part of China's "opening to the world" the government created several Special Economic Zones along the eastern coast. Because of their location on the Pacific Rim, these Special Economic Zones have increased trade connections[1] with other countries. Chinese and foreign-owned companies in these cities pay less taxes. They are often given land to build new factories and industries. This encourages rapid development. Shenzhen is a Special Economic Zone.

Hong Kong is already the most developed area of China. It is one of the world's most important trade and business centers. Hong Kong companies produce goods exported around the world.

MIDDLE LEFT: Seaports in the Special Economic Zones are very busy.

TOP RIGHT: New high rise towers contain the offices of many foreign companies.

2ND RIGHT: Shenzhen has many clothing factories.

3RD RIGHT: Production of silk is a traditional skill in China. Today China is a leading producer of silk fabric.

BOTTOM RIGHT: Computers are becoming common in offices and businesses throughout China.

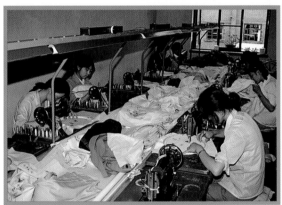

China's Main Exports
- textiles (cloth or material)
- clothing
- footwear
- toys
- machinery and equipment

China's Main Imports
- steel
- motor vehicles
- textile machinery
- oil products
- aircraft and parts

---

[1]See China's major trade partners, page 29.

Interior Development

Today, China's eastern coast is more developed than the **interior** areas. The largest cities are located along the eastern coast.[1] These cities have the best transportation and communication systems in China. They also have good education and health facilities. Most factories and industries are located along the coast. People have more choices of jobs, housing, shopping, and entertainment than in the countryside. Wages are also higher.

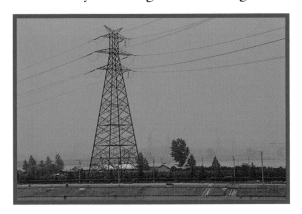

The government plans to develop the interior areas of the country to the same level as the coast. To do this, natural resources need to be developed. New transportation and communication systems must be built. A hydroelectric dam is being built across the Chang Jiang to provide more electricity.

New industries require electrical energy to power machinery. Communications equipment needs electricity. People will use more power to run the new appliances they have in their homes.

Natural Resources

The interior areas are rich in minerals, oil, and natural gas.[2] Rivers in the interior are good sources for hydroelectric power. The government is using foreign technology and money to develop these natural resources.

Protecting the Environment

China wants to develop new industries and natural resources to improve people's lives. They also wish to preserve and protect the environment. New rules limit the air and water pollution caused by industries. The government has closed some factories and lumber mills that caused severe air or water pollution. New sewage treatment plants are being built to reduce pollution from cities. Logged areas are now replanted with trees. Wildlife conservation projects protect endangered wildlife such as the Giant Panda.

TOP LEFT: Hydroelectric lines carry power to cities, villages, and factories.

TOP RIGHT: Factories and industries often produce air and water pollution.

MIDDLE RIGHT: In China, as elsewhere in the world, pollution damages the environment.

ABOVE AND BOTTOM RIGHT: The Giant Panda lives on bamboo, but bamboo forests are being reduced due to development.

interior—inner, away from the coast
[1] See Population Density map page 107.
[2] See Natural Resources map in mini-atlas (inside end sheets)

THE NEW CHINA

The Three Gorges Dam

The Chang Jiang (Yangtze River) flows 6300 kilometers across China from the Tibetan Plateau to the Pacific Ocean. Only the Amazon and Nile rivers are longer then the Chang Jiang.

For thousands of years, the Chang Jiang has been a main transportation route across China. Today large ocean-going ships can travel upstream as far as Wuhan. Smaller ships can reach Chongqing.

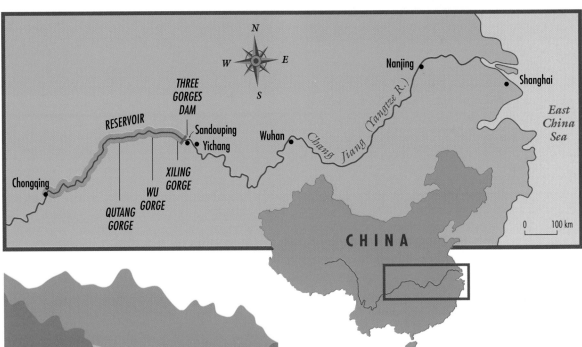

Water level will rise. Towns and villages will be submerged.

In 1993 the Chinese government began to build a hydroelectric dam across the Chang Jiang near the Three Gorges. This huge project will bring many changes. When the dam is built, it will hold back the river water. The river upsteam will become deeper, gradually flooding the valley. It will form an artificial lake, or reservoir, in the river valley, as shown in the map and 3-D model on this page.

When completed in 2009 the Three Gorges Dam will be the largest hydro-electric project ever built.

The dam will create a new lake stretching for 500 kilometers upstream from Sandouping to Chongqing. The water level above the dam will rise 100 meters, covering 13 cities, 140 towns, 1500 factories, and thousands of hectares of farmland. Over one million people will need to be resettled elsewhere.

Reasons for the Dam

The Three Gorges Dam will provide benefits.
- The yearly flooding of the Chang Jiang that kills thousands of people and destroys property and farmland will be controlled.
- Electricity for new industries and homes will be generated.
- China's output of **carbon dioxide** and **sulfur dioxide** will be reduced. (Without the dam, more coal-powered electricity plants would be needed. Coal-powered plants release millions of tonnes of carbon dioxide and sulfur dioxide into the atmosphere.)
- The Chang Jiang will be improved as a transportation route, allowing large ocean-going ships to travel as far as Chongqing.

Opposition to the Dam

Some Chinese environment experts and world environment groups believe the Three Gorges Dam will have disastrous effects on wildlife, fishing, and farming.
- 75 million people who farm or fish along the Chang Jiang may not be able to make a living there. They will need to move or seek other employment.
- Farmland upstream from the dam will be under water.
- Without the **silt** from the yearly floods, farmland below the dam may not produce good crops.
- River fishing may be reduced; currently 50% of China's freshwater fish are caught in the Chang Jiang.
- Tonnes of silt and rocks carried by the river may clog the **generators** at the dam and eventually fill the lake behind the dam.
- Wildlife such as river dolphin may not survive.

carbon dioxide—a gas produced from burning and other processes, contributing to global warming
sulfur dioxide—a chemical responsible for acid rain when it mixes with water in the atmosphere
silt—fine particles of earth carried by a river, dropped to form layers of soil
generators—machines that produce electrical energy

DRAGON RIVER

Zhou Bin trudged down the steep trail that wound from the mountain top to the village on the river bank. His woven sandals kicked up clouds of dust along the stony trail. The heavy hoe and wicker basket tied to his back bumped against his tired shoulders. His father, two uncles, and several cousins were following slowly behind him. Zhou Bin stopped on the trail and squatted back on his heels to rest. It was long, hot work building the new terraces. Rocks had to be dug from the hard ground and piled to form a wall. Then the hillside was dug away to form a narrow shelf. Next spring the new terraces would be planted with tangerine and orange trees.

Every day, Zhou Bin and all the members of his family worked building new terraces. The terraces needed to be ready by next year. Their village, the orchards of oranges, tangerines, peaches and their fields of sweet potatoes were going to be covered by the new lake created by the Three Gorges Dam. The entire valley would be flooded. Half the city of WanXian a few kilometers upriver would be under water. Over 100 000 city residents would need to move to new homes. From where he sat, Zhou Bin could see the white wooden signs with the red lines dotting the hillside across the river. The signs showed how high the Chang Jiang would be once the dam was completed.

The Communist Party Secretary came last week to explain the government plans to pay farmers whose fields and homes would be flooded by the new lake. She explained that the government would build new homes, roads, and factories, and install power lines. She told them about the villages that had already moved to new homes. They had electricity, televisions, and a more comfortable life. They could work in the new factories or help with the road building and construction jobs in the area. They had new opportunities to improve their lives.

Zhou Bin stared at the ribbon of river while he listened to his relatives discuss the government's plans. He found it difficult to imagine a huge lake in place of the narrow river valley. His family had always lived along the Chang Jiang, cultivating the hillsides, marrying, and raising their families. A shining lake instead of this great river seemed impossible to imagine.

Here the Chang Jiang curled peacefully between the mountain slopes. Villages dotted the hillsides. Terraces, orchards, and rice paddies spread out from the villages. Narrow dirt trails wound up and across the hillsides. There were no highways. Everything moved on foot along the dirt trails or was transported along the river.

THE NEW CHINA

The villagers worried that the new terraces high on the mountain slopes would not be as productive as those lower down. The fishing families worried that the dam would kill the river fish and they would not be able to make a living. Grandmother worried about moving the family tombs higher up the slope out of the reach of the river waters. So many worries and so many decisions to make.

As usual, the river below them was crowded with traffic. Several narrow fishing boats fought the strong current along the shoreline. Village families made a good living fishing and selling the fish at the local markets. A small ferry that carried people across the river was unloading baskets of oranges, walnuts, and a few pigs. A small boat towing a barge carrying steel pipe came speeding down the river, pushed along by the swift current. Struggling up the river against the current was an open boat stacked with baskets of fruit and charcoal headed for WanXian.

This was the great river. It was the longest, most important river in China. When it was flooded with the rains it roared through the gorges, churning and frothing with frightening currents. It was easy to imagine it as an angry dragon roaring its way from the distant mountains to the ocean. Soon the river would be a tamed, flat lake. Zhou Bin wondered how the river dragon would like having its freedom controlled by the new dam.

As he watched the familiar activity on the river, Zhou Bin thought about the plans, decisions, and work that lay ahead. The possibilities were both frightening and exciting. He had never considered any other life but working here, farming with his uncles and cousins. Now, he could consider a factory or construction job. Like everyone in the village, Zhou Bin worried about how the dam would change their lives.

Zhou Bin sighed and stood up to continue the hike home. Like the great river below, his mind seemed to be rushing and swirling in circles. There were so many changes ahead for his family, his village, and the river. Just like the great river, Zhou Bin knew that once the dam was finished his life and the lives of all the villagers in the valley would never be the same.

FOOD

Chinese meals consist mainly of grains and vegetables. Large amounts of meat, fish, or **dairy products** are usually not part of the regular diet. Rice is primarily eaten in the south and wheat products in the north.

The Chinese were the first to grow tea bushes and produce tea. Thermoses filled with hot water are always available in family kitchens, offices, and hotel rooms to make tea throughout the day.

Chinese meals of rice and vegetables are popular in North America and Europe because it is a healthy way to eat.

Cooking Methods

Chinese cooking is done in a wok or a bamboo steamer over a small stove. These cooking methods use less fuel or energy than cooking in an oven.

Woks are used to prepare soup, deep-fry, steam, and **stir-fry** food. Stir-frying is popular in North America. This quick cooking method keeps **nutrients** in food so it is more healthful.

Meat, dumplings, vegetables, and buns can be steam cooked using a bamboo steamer and a wok. A bamboo steamer is placed over the water in the wok. The steam from the boiling water cooks the food inside the steamer.

dairy products—products made from milk such as cheese, ice cream, yogurt
stir-fry—small pieces of meat and vegetables quickly stirred in a very hot wok
nutrients—vitamins and minerals

Eating Styles

Many eating customs and traditions in China are very old. Chopsticks have been used in China for over 3000 years. Tables are often round so everyone is the same distance from food platters placed in the center. Chopsticks and soup spoons are used in place of knives and forks. Food is piled on top of rice in the rice bowl. Bringing the rice bowl close to your mouth and using the chopsticks or a soup spoon to scoop food into it is the usual way to eat.

Regional Cooking Styles

Northern Style (found near Beijing): Wheat noodles, steamed breads, pancakes, and dumplings are featured in Northern dishes. Mongolian and Muslim people also eat lamb meat, garlic, and vinegar. A famous Northern dish is "Peking Duck." Roasted duck meat is finely sliced, wrapped in thin pancakes, and eaten with plum sauce and onions.

Sichuan Style (found near Chengdu): Dishes are spiced with hot chilies, red pepper, black beans, ginger, garlic, and sesame paste. Chilies were introduced by European traders 400 years ago and added to Sichuan dishes. A typical Sichuan dish is chicken simmered in soy sauce, onions, garlic, and bean curd. Peanuts, hot chilies, and sesame paste give added flavor.

Eastern Style (found around Shanghai): Dishes use a variety of seafood, vegetables, and fruit from the region. A special dish consists of stuffing chicken with pork, vegetables, and spices and then cooking it in a clay container.

Cantonese Style (found near Guangzhou, Shenzhen, and Hong Kong): This is the best known cooking style outside China. A wide variety of meats, fish, and seafood are flavored with oyster or plum sauces and shrimp paste. Tiny dumplings with various fillings, called *dim sum*, are a Cantonese favorite.

How to Use Chopsticks

1. Place one chopstick in the crook of the thumb and rest the end on the tip of your ring finger.

2. Place the top chopstick between your thumb and your first two fingers.

3. Keep the bottom chopstick steady. Move the top chopstick up and down using your thumb and index finger.

THE NEW CHINA

Changing Foods

In the last few years there have been changes in the usual diet, largely because of technology. Improved transportation systems, changing farming methods, and refrigeration have all affected the foods that are available. More fast foods are also being sold in China.

1 People in cities are eating more food and different kinds of food than in the past. Many young people are giving up the healthy traditional diet for a diet higher in fat and sugar.

2 Many people in large cities like Hong Kong and Shenzhen are eating more meat, fish, and eggs. Dairy products, such as milk, cheese, and ice cream are eaten more often. In some well-off areas, people can afford meat, fish, or eggs every day. This is a change from the traditional meals of rice and vegetables.

3 In the past, people shopped daily. Now that more families own refrigerators, many people shop only a few times a week. Quick snacks and packaged meals are also replacing daily shopping for fresh goods.

4 A better transportation system allows fresh fruit and vegetables to be shipped to North China during the winter. In the past, people in the north depended on cabbage, potatoes, and radishes as their traditional winter vegetables. Today a wide selection of vegetables and fruit are grown year round in greenhouses.

飲食改善

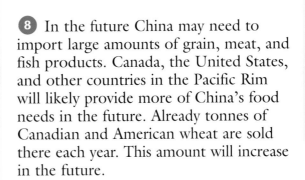

5 People in cities are eating more **processed food**. Supermarkets and street markets sell a wide variety of familiar North American products.

6 Western fast foods such as donuts, hamburgers, pizza, and fried chicken are available in large cities. Chocolate, ice cream, potato chips, cookies, and soft drinks are popular snacks.

7 As the demand for beef and pork increases more land must be used to grow corn and wheat to feed pigs and cattle. This means less land is available to produce food for the huge population.

8 In the future China may need to import large amounts of grain, meat, and fish products. Canada, the United States, and other countries in the Pacific Rim will likely provide more of China's food needs in the future. Already tonnes of Canadian and American wheat are sold there each year. This amount will increase in the future.

9 North American companies hope that China's young people will develop a taste for North American foods.

processed food—food products prepared in factories; not fresh

HAVING FUN!

Chinese people enjoy many traditional **leisure time** activities. Technology has added new choices for how people spend their free time.

Television

Televisions are now common. Distant areas of the country receive television signals by satellite. People living in small villages can now find out what is happening in China and the world. Many people take education courses or practice their English through television. However, the government strictly controls what can be broadcast. News stories must be approved by the government.

Movies

Movies are very popular. As part of China's "opening to the world," foreign movies can be shown. They must first be approved by the government. Chinese-made movies have won international film competitions. They are now shown around the world.

Kites

Kites were invented in China thousands of years ago. Both children and adults enjoy flying kites as a leisure activity. Many cities have annual kite-flying competitions or special days. Thousands come to parks to fly their kites.

Computers

Only very well-off families can afford the expense of a computer. Only a small number are connected to the internet.

Chinese Writing

Practicing calligraphy is a favorite pastime. Learning to make the strokes for each character perfectly takes hours of practice. Special rice paper, brushes, and blocks of dry ink are used in the art of calligraphy.

Chinese Opera

Chinese opera is a type of entertainment enjoyed by many people. Chinese opera relies mainly on singing and dancing to tell stories. Characters wear elaborate costumes and make-up. Performances of Chinese opera are regularly shown on television.

Music

Listening to music is a popular leisure activity in China. Traditional and popular Chinese music are commonly heard there, as well as classical and popular music from North America and Europe. Most people listen to the radio because tickets to live performances are very expensive.

leisure time—time not spent in school or work; time to relax and do hobbies

Song Birds

Raising song birds is a favorite pastime of older men. Every morning bird owners bring their birds to neighborhood parks for fresh air. Their birds learn songs from other birds. Cages and song birds are sold at Hong Kong's bird market.

Sports

Traditional Chinese sports and modern Western sports are popular activities for children and adults. Students learn a variety of sports at an early age. There are many sports centers where youngsters live, attend school, exercise, and train. Eventually they may play for one of the national sports teams.

China's athletes have won an impressive number of medals in a wide variety of sports at recent Olympic Games.

Soccer, **table tennis**, volleyball, swimming, gymnastics, and basketball are popular with adults and children. Table tennis is often considered China's national sport because so many people play it.

In cities traditional **martial arts** are very popular activities. *Wushu*, *taijiquan* and *qigong* are some common ways of keeping fit and healthy.

Taijiquan (often called *tai chi*) is one of the most popular martial arts exercises in China. The movements are designed to keep the body flexible and develop balance and concentration. At dawn people in China gather in groups in parks and streets to practice this exercise. Many North Americans and Europeans take *taijiquan* classes.

table tennis—ping pong
martial arts—skills once used by soldiers to practice self-defense and by monks to improve their concentration
wushu—a martial art also known as *kung fu*
qigong—a type of healing exercise

THE NEW CHINA

FESTIVALS

For thousands of years the people of China have celebrated many special days each year called **festivals**. Some new festivals they celebrate today are
- International Working Women's Day (8 March)
- Arbor Day (12 March)
- Chinese Youth Day (4 May)
- International Children's Day (1 June)
- Army Day (1 August)
- International Labor Day (1 May)
- Teachers' Day (10 September)
- National Day (1 October).

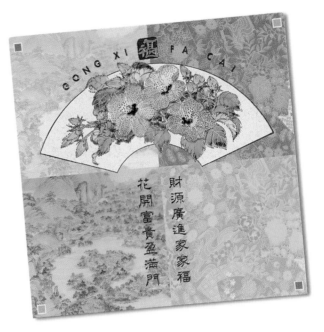

Spring Festival

(Chinese New Year)

Spring Festival has been celebrated in China for more than 3000 years. It is still the most popular festival.

On the Chinese **lunar calendar** Spring Festival marks the end of winter and the start of a new year. The lunar calendar follows the cycles of the moon, with 13 months in the year.[1] Chinese New Year is usually celebrated near the end of January or the beginning of February.

The Spring Festival is an important family holiday. People travel hundreds of kilometers to be home for Spring Festival.

Families clean the graves of ancestors, visit relatives and friends, exchange New Year cards, and eat special foods wrapped in red paper. Children are often given money tucked into red envelopes. Homes are decorated with lucky sayings printed on red paper. People welcome the new year with dragon dances and fireworks.

Each year of the Chinese calendar is named after an animal. There are 12 years in the cycle. People are thought to take on the characteristics of the animal representing the year of their birth.

ABOVE: A New Year's money gift envelope

TOP RIGHT: A New Year's greeting card

BOTTOM: Bright colors and big parades are part of celebration in both China and North America.

---

[1]After 1911 China adopted a calendar containing 12 months.

Lantern Festival

The Lantern Festival officially marks the end of the Spring Festival. Multicolored lanterns and fireworks light up the night sky during the festival. Children parade with lanterns made in shapes of goldfish, dragons, birds, or red globes.

Mid-Autumn Festival

The Mid-Autumn Festival is held about the middle of September to celebrate the harvest. Families visit relatives, celebrate the full autumn moon, and eat round, sweet "moon cakes" stuffed with dates and nuts.

Dragon Boat Festival

The beginning of the summer is celebrated with the dragon boat festival and races. Long wooden boats with dragon heads and tails are powered by teams of rowers. Dragon boat racing has become very popular in other Asian countries and in North America.

National Day

National Day is held each year to celebrate October 1, 1949, the day Mao Zedong announced the start of the People's Republic of China. Parades, fireworks, and dances are held all over China. The biggest celebration is in Tiananmen Square in Beijing.

Harbin Snow Festival

Harbin, in northern China, holds a snow festival in mid-winter. Artists carve blocks of ice into animals, characters from stories, palaces, and wonderful dragons. Some years, artists have carved a "Great Wall" from ice.

LOOKING BACK

Activities

Impressions (pages 114–117)

1. **Look** carefully at the photographs on pages 114–117.
   a) **Classify** them into the three types of needs and wants.
   b) **Develop** possible responses to the eight questions listed on page 113.

Geography (pages 56–57)

1. ➡ **Mark** the following on your map of China:
   • The Three Gorges Dam project at Sandouping between Chongqing and Wuhan

Communications (pages 118–119)

1. Using information you have gathered about China's government, **write** a short paragraph explaining why the Chinese government wants to control information on television, in newspapers, and on the internet.

2. Make a **list** of the new communications technology that is now available in China. **Write** five statements explaining how this new technology may change life in China.

Transportation (pages 120–121)

1. **Write** ten statements about transportation in China. Include traditional and modern methods of transportation used there and how new transportation technologies (railways, highways, airlines, subways) might affect life in China.

Development (pages 122–127)

1. **Review** the geography of the three regions of China explored in this text. Make a **list** showing how features of China's geography affect coastal and interior development.

2. **Explain** why energy is important to the development of a country.

3. Imagine you are a geographer reading the narrative Dragon River on pages 126–127 of the text. Make a **list** of information about the Three Gorges Dam and its effects on people and the environment contained in the narrative.

4. **Write** an imaginary dialog between a government official supporting the Three Gorges Dam and an opponent of the dam. Use information from page 125 to develop your arguments.

5. **Create** a model of the Three Gorges Dam illustrating the river level in the valley and the new lake formed by the dam.

6. Many of the things North Americans use every day are made in Chinese factories. Look around your home and school. Make a **list** of clothing items or other items that have a "Made in China" label. **Compare** lists with other students. What conclusions can be made from the items on the lists?

7. **Prepare** a presentation (see page 147 for ideas) to show the following: What can we learn from the Chinese about development? What can they learn from us?

Food (pages 128–131)

1. **Create** a poster illustrating regional cooking styles.

2. **Compare** what a teenager in China might eat in a typical day with what a North American teenager might eat.

3. With classmates, **organize** and **prepare** a Chinese meal. Include as many regional cooking styles as possible.

Having Fun! (pages 132–133)

1. Make a **list** showing how technology has changed recreational activities in China in recent years.

2. Hold a special kite **making** session and kite flying **competition**.

Festivals (pages 134–135)

1. **Create** a one-year timeline highlighting several of China's favorite festivals and holidays.

2. **Organize** a Chinese festival day in your class. Decide which festival to celebrate and then **prepare** materials, food, and activities to match that festival.

Chapter Review

1. Use one of the strategies on page 142 for **recording** or adding information to the following vocabulary: development, Special Economic Zones, trade. Put this assignment in the WordBook section of your China binder.

2. **Create** and **present** a word poster with one of the chapter's vocabulary terms. Word posters are described in the Appendix on page 144.

3. **Classify** the photographs in this chapter into
   • physical, psychological, and group needs
   • physical, psychological, and group wants

4. **Check** the organization of your activities for this chapter in your binder:
   • chapter title page, notes, activities, maps, and illustrations in Activities section
   • definitions in WordBook section
   • China Journal writings
   • Tools of Learning notes

5. Do either a) or b).
   a) **Summarize** your research notes for this chapter into a retrieval chart. Either make your own chart or ask your teacher for a summary chart for this chapter.
   b) **Answer** Taylor's questions on page 113.

6. When you have finished reading about Taylor's visit to Shenzhen and Hong Kong, **write** your own captions for the photographs on pages 114–117. Do not write in the textbook. Include information you learned in the chapter.

7. Imagine you are with Taylor. Before you left home you promised to send your family and friends some news from China. **Select** and **prepare** one of the following for your message about Shenzhen and/or Hong Kong. Include three facts and three impressions or personal feelings.
   • cartoon/ comic strip
   • illustrated poem
   • letter
   • drawing
   • e-mail message
   • postcard
   • story

8. **Create** a game about development along China's east coast. Include at least 10 facts from pages 118–127.

9. Encourage North Americans to visit Hong Kong by **creating** one of the following:
   • booklet
   • pamphlet
   • display
   • travel brochure
   • magazine or newspaper article
   • exhibition

10. In question 1 on page 31 under Government you started a **web** showing how the Chinese government influences or controls the way the people live. Add information from this chapter to this web.

The Way Home

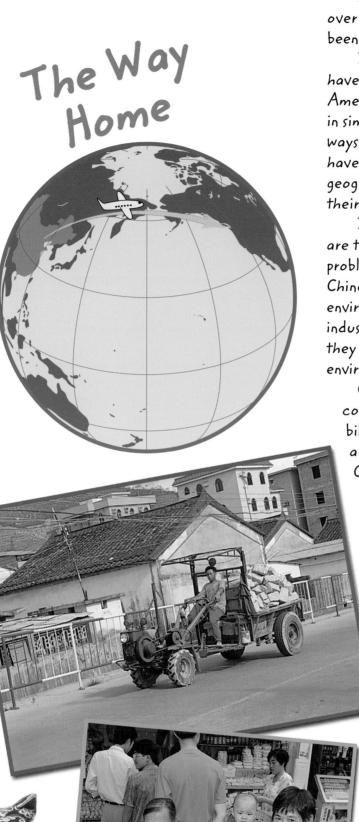

It's hard to believe the China trip is over and we're on our way home. It has been a terrific trip.

I've discovered that people in China have the same needs as we do in North America. Sometimes we meet our needs in similar ways and sometimes in different ways. After seeing China on this trip I have a better understanding of how geography affects the ways people meet their needs.

I found out that the people in China are trying to solve some of the same problems we are in North America. Chinese people are worried about the environment. They want to develop industries, run cars, live in cities, but they want to preserve the natural environment, too.

China's huge population is a special concern for their government. Over a billion people is a lot to feed, house, and educate. I wonder if the One-Child Family Plan will work?

I found out how the movement of people to the cities and new technology has changed how people meet their needs. A change of lifestyles creates conflicts between new technology and traditional ways of doing things. The Chinese want the new technology, but they also want to keep their traditions and customs. This often happens in North America, also.

I think that sharing ideas, technology, and ways of doing things could help solve problems among the countries of the Pacific Rim. In the past China made many valuable contributions to the world, such as printing. Before the China trip I didn't realize that some of the things we use in everyday life were first discovered or invented in China.

I expected China to be like the photographs in my school library books. The China we saw on this trip has been very different. I put a few of my favorite photographs on this last page. Whenever I look at this journal and photographs I'll be reminded of what I learned about China.

I'm really looking forward to showing my family and friends my photographs, sketches, and journal. I'm really pleased with my journal. That's definitely one thing I learned on this trip. Research and writing are hard work but being a journalist and traveling to different countries is great!

I can't wait to get home and see my family. I'm also looking forward to calling my friends, watching my favorite television shows, and going out to my favorite restaurant. I am especially looking forward to sleeping in my own bed!

歸途

LOOKING BACK

Activities

1. a) While studying China you learned about the following topics.

How do the Chinese people meet their needs and wants?

How is technology changing life in China?

How do traditions and customs affect how the Chinese people meet their needs?

How does life in China compare with life where you live?

How are the countries of the Pacific Rim becoming increasingly interdependent?

As a conclusion to your study of China you are to **communicate** what you've learned to the other students in your class. (You may wish to put on a China Day and invite other students and/or your parents to view what you've learned about China.) See page 147 of the Appendix for presentation ideas.

Start by going through your China binder—especially the section called Activities. Select interesting activities that present the most information to show to others. Also select activities that you did such as models, charts, murals, dioramas, and paintings that portray life in China. Include something on each of the five topics listed on this page.

1. b) Research Project

If you did a research project on China, **complete** the second and third parts of the research project model that follows. This model is explained in more detail on page 142.

Gathering Information

Examining and Organizing Information

Presenting the Information

Options for Presentation

Your conclusions for the topics on page 140 will be based on the research you carried out on China. Presenting such a large amount of information is best done in groups so the tasks can be split among a number of people. The information can be presented in many ways. A group may wish to use a combination of methods that suit the information they are presenting and the preferences of the group members.

Some ways you can communicate your projects follow. Select and prepare some of these presentation methods.

booklet	multimedia
cartoon	mural
chart	newspaper article
collage	oral report
collection	pamphlet
comic strip	panel discussion
debate	pictures
diagram	play
diary	poster
diorama	radio show
display	role-play/drama
drawings	scrapbook
exhibition	scroll
fact file	television news
flow chart	show
graph	timeline
interview	top 10 list
letter	web page
magazine article	written report
mobile	

Additional ideas for presentations are found in the Appendix on page 147.

APPENDIX

 ## Research Project

There are many different ways to do projects. This model is suggested for studying China.

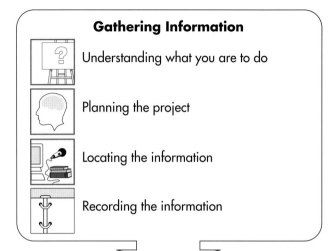

Gathering Information

- Understanding what you are to do
- Planning the project
- Locating the information
- Recording the information

Examining and Organizing Information

- Examining the information
- Organizing the information

Presenting the Information

- Concluding the project
- Presenting the project to others
- Evaluating what you've done

Learning How to Learn (SKIMM™)

On the following pages you will find a variety of ideas for making notes, answering questions, and doing activities. Add to or delete from the sample organizers as needed.

 ## Recording Vocabulary

Create your own glossary. Use one of the following ways of recording vocabulary or design your own.

Method 1: Word Charts

Word Write the new vocabulary term here.		Picture Draw a simple sketch of the word to help you remember its meaning. Color this sketch. You are not expected to create something artistic and no one will see this drawing unless you want them to.
Meaning Write out the meaning in your own words. Use the information in the textbook, in the glossary, or from a dictionary to help you better understand the meaning.	**Example** Write out examples from China to show how the word is used.	
Word		**Picture**
Meaning	**Example**	

Method 2: New Words

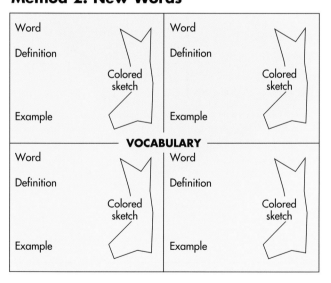

NOTE: Registered™ 1996 Arnold Publishing Ltd. SKIMM™ (Skills, Models, and Methods) Learning How to Learn—the technique of assigning questions/activities written in a textbook or digital presentation and referring users to an appendix or glossary (print or digital) for suggestions on how to carry it out has been registered as a trademark by Arnold Publishing Ltd. All copy used in SKIMM™ (Learning How to Learn), including the icons, is protected by copyright. ©1996 and ©1998 Arnold Publishing Ltd.

An expansion of SKIMM™ (Learning How to Learn) is available on the *China* homepage of the Arnold Publishing internet site. See page v for details.

Note Making

Method 1: T-Notes

T-Notes consist of a combination of written notes and drawings. Use the following format or design your own.

Main title Write one or two sentences to describe what this section is about.	
Drawing or sketch	Sub-titles –write notes in point form here

Example
(Refer to pages 10–11 in *China*.)

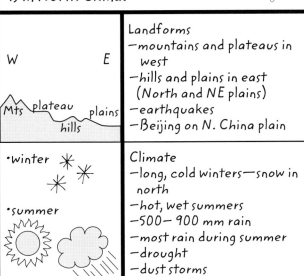

Geography of North China
China divided into three regions: North, West, South based on elevation and climate. Beijing is in North China.

W E Mts plateau plains hills	Landforms –mountains and plateaus in west –hills and plains in east (North and NE plains) –earthquakes –Beijing on N. China plain
•winter •summer	Climate –long, cold winters—snow in north –hot, wet summers –500–900 mm rain –most rain during summer –drought –dust storms

Method 2: Webs

Also called clustering, this type of graphic organizer is used to:
- generate ideas, as in **brainstorming**
- illustrate ideas (by using words and/or simple drawings)
- link ideas
- take notes

Colored drawings may be added to webs to aid memory.

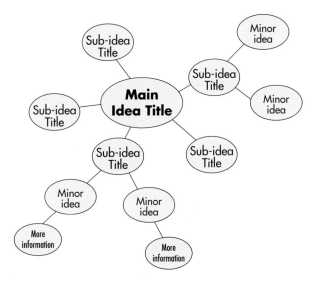

Example
(Refer to pages 10–12 in *China*.)

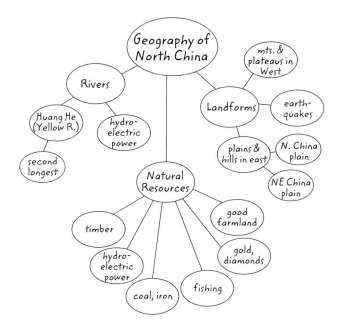

brainstorming—a strategy of thinking of as many ideas about a topic as possible

Word Poster

Word posters are a fun way to learn, remember new information, and share what you've learned with your classmates. Word posters may be done individually, in pairs, or as a small group. A word poster is more than a visual display. To create one, follow these steps:

Step 1: Once you have selected a vocabulary term or a topic, read about it in your textbook and review any information you have about it in your China binder.

Step 2: Plan and create a visual representation of your word or topic by including one or more of the following:

music/song	poem
picture (photo, drawing, map, or diagram)	rap
	skit
	words

Step 3: Present your word poster to your classmates. You may either tell them what word or topic you are presenting or get them to guess.

Making Charts and Graphic Organizers

Charts are also referred to as diagrams, tables, or graphs. Charts are used as a quick way to organize and record information.

Graphic organizers are learning tools to help you organize your thinking. They provide an overview of what you are studying. Graphic organizers usually show relationships. Examples follow on pages 144–146.

Retrieval Chart

Title		
Criteria	**A**	**B**

List items or criteria you are describing.

Record important information as it relates to the criteria.

Example

The following retrieval chart organizes one's notes on transportation and homes.

Basic Needs Chart		
Physical Needs	China	Where I Live
trans-portation	−bicycle common −human power to haul goods −only few people own cars −parking a problem −pollution from cars & trucks a problem −new freeways & highways	−bikes mainly for kids −little human power used −families often own more than one car −some teenagers own cars −lots of parking & homes have garages −pollution from cars & trucks a problem −new freeways & highways
homes	−small, simple −few luxuries −most live in apartments in cities	−quite large −many rooms −some apartments, some houses in cities

 **Making Charts and Graphic Organizers (continued)**

Flow Charts
Flow charts are sequential diagrams that show classification, relationships, possibilities, or choices.

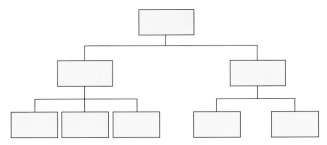

Classification Using a Flow Chart
Classification is a commonly used thinking tool. To classify you are gathering together ideas, events, or items and arranging them into groups that have common characteristics.

Steps Involved in Classifying
1. Randomly list items or examples.
2. Identify and label groups (categories) based on their characteristics.
3. Sort into groups based on similarities.
4. (optional) Record information on a graphic organizer.

Example
Using the photographs and their captions on pages 8–9 classify their contents into needs and wants.

Step 1: Randomly list items or examples.

bike	self-esteem
car	friendship
clothing	cell phone
work	McDonald's
food	Pizza Hut
jewelry	Hard Rock Cafe
government	stylish clothing
home	brand name shoes
new apartment	transportation

Step 2: Identify and label groups (categories) based on their characteristics.

<u>Group 1: Needs</u>   <u>Group 2: Wants</u>

Step 3: Sort into groups based on similarities.

<u>Needs</u>	<u>Wants</u>
transportation	fancy bike
clothing	car
home	stylish clothing
work	brand name shoes
self-esteem	jewelry
friendship	new apartment
government	cell phone
food	eat at McDonald's, Pizza Hut, Hard Rock Cafe

Step 4: Record information on a graphic organizer.

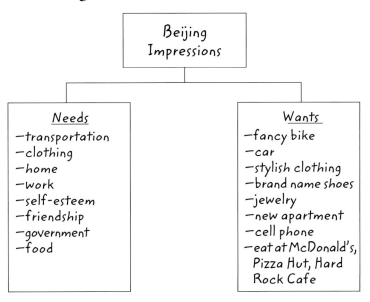

Note: Because each of us thinks differently, there are many ways to classify information. The example on this page and the flow chart show one way to do this.

Making Charts and Graphic Organizers (continued)

Several charts can be used for comparing (showing similarities and differences).

Comparison Chart

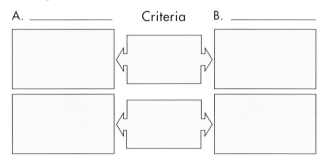

A. _____   Criteria   B. _____

Comparison Using a Comparison Chart

This thinking tool is used to show how something is similar to and different from something else.

Steps Involved in Comparing

1. Identify what you are comparing.
2. Identify what criteria you are going to use to compare them.
3. Show how the items you are comparing are the same and how they are different based on the criteria you identified.

   Charts are a useful way to show comparisons.

Example

Step 1: Identify what you are comparing.

A.   China   CITY HOMES   B. Where I Live

Step 2: Identify what criteria you are going to use to compare them.

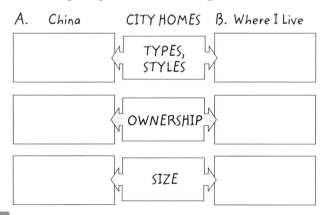

A.   China   CITY HOMES   B. Where I Live

TYPES, STYLES

OWNERSHIP

SIZE

Step 3: Show how the items you are comparing are the same and how they are different based on the criteria you identified.

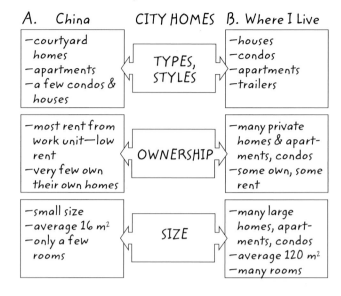

A.   China   CITY HOMES   B. Where I Live

| TYPES, STYLES | —courtyard homes —apartments —a few condos & houses | —houses —condos —apartments —trailers |

| OWNERSHIP | —most rent from work unit—low rent —very few own their own homes | —many private homes & apartments, condos —some own, some rent |

| SIZE | —small size —average 16 m² —only a few rooms | —many large homes, apartments, condos —average 120 m² —many rooms |

Venn Diagram

Topic: _____

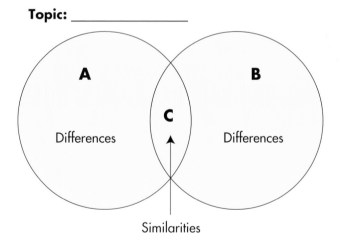

A — Differences

C

B — Differences

Similarities

Comparison Using a Venn Diagram

1. Identify what topic and what two areas (A and B) you are comparing.
2. Identify (and keep in your mind) what criteria you are going to use to show differences. In circle A write words or descriptions about the criteria you selected. Do the same for circle B.
3. In the central space C randomly list ways in which A and B are the same.

Example

Topic: Transportation

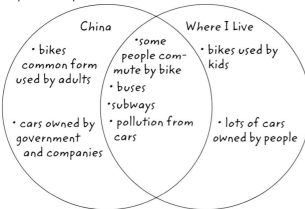

China
- bikes common form used by adults
- cars owned by government and companies

some people commute by bike
- buses
- subways
- pollution from cars

Where I Live
- bikes used by kids
- lots of cars owned by people

Presentations

To prepare and carry out a presentation follow these steps:

Step 1: In making a presentation you must first select one main topic or idea as a focus for your presentation. Everything you do in your presentation must be related to or provide examples of this main idea.

Step 2: Select a method of presentation from the list to the right and find out from your teacher or the library how you are to make or prepare it. For example, if you are making a diorama you first have to find out what it is and how to make it.[1]

Step 3: Read about your topic or idea in the textbook and review any information you have about it in your China research notes.

Step 4: Plan on paper how you are going to prepare the presentation you selected. Establish criteria on how to judge your presentation.

Step 5: Prepare the presentation on the topic or idea you selected.

Step 6: Present your topic or idea to your classmates. Judge your presentation based on the criteria from Step 4.

Some Ideas

advertisement
banner
booklet
cartoon
charades
chart
collage
collection
comic strip
construction
cooking
  demonstration
dance
debate
demonstration
diagram
diary
diorama
display
drawing
exhibition
fact file
fairy tale
flow chart
game
game board/cards
graph
illustrated poem
interview
job description
letter
magazine
map
mask
mime
mobile
model
mosaic
multimedia
  presentation

mural
music
newspaper
newspaper article
oral report
painting
pamphlet
panel discussion
papier-mâché
photo album
photographs
picture
play
poem
poster
project cube
project triangle
puppet show
puzzle
questionnaire
radio show
rap
riddles
role-play/drama
scrapbook
scroll
sculpture
skit
slide/tape show
song
stories
talk show
television show
timeline (illustrated)
top 10 list
web page
word poster
written report

---

[1]Check the Arnold website at http://www.arnold.ca/ for presentation ideas. See page v for details.

GLOSSARY

The number in brackets following the words refers to the page on which the word first appears in bold type. The word may be defined in the paragraph on the page or at the bottom of the page.

abacus (76)—a frame with beads used for calculating

acupuncture (53)—a medical treatment developed in China; needles are inserted into specific areas of the body

altar (46)—a raised place or small table used in religious ceremonies

arthritis (81)—a disease causing swelling and pain in joints

autonomous region (44)—a region of China that has some self-government, where members of minority nationalities keep their own language, customs, and traditional lifestyles

banned (118)—not allowed

bargain (71)—discuss a selling price

basic needs (3)— human requirements that must be satisfied to avoid discomfort, pain, or even death; includes physical, psychological, and group needs

basin (38)—an area of low land surrounded by higher land

bazaar (40)—a large market area often with covered stalls

BCE (20)—Before the Common Era, equivalent to BC

bean curd (13)—tofu; a form of food made from soybeans

Bible (47)—the holy book of Christianity

brainstorming (143)—a strategy of thinking of as many ideas about a topic as possible

brazier (62)—a stand for holding lighted coals or fire

Buddha (39)—founder of the Buddhist religion

Buddhism (47)—a religion brought to China from India, based on the teachings of the Buddha

calligraphy (78)—writing Chinese characters using special brushes and ink

canal (56)—an artificial waterway

candidate (28)—person who is seeking a position or office

canola (35)—a plant grown for oil made from seeds

caravan (32)—a group of people traveling with pack horses, camels, or donkeys

carbon dioxide (125)—a gas produced from burning and other processes, contributing to global warming

casting iron (48)—heating iron to high temperatures until molten and then pouring it into molds

CE (20)—Common Era, equivalent to AD

central heating (13)—a furnace or boiler that provides heat to all the rooms of a building or apartment through pipes

characters (78)—line pictures that represent objects or ideas

chemicals (81)—basic substances that may be combined to make other substances

Christianity (47)—a religion that follows the teachings of Christ recorded in the Bible

citizen (76)—an inhabitant of a country

climate (11)—description of the usual weather conditions of a place over a long period of time

clinic (52)—a medical office dealing with minor illnesses and injuries

commune (64)—a large government-owned farm

communication (78)—the giving or exchange of information

Communist (23)—a political system where the resources of the country are shared equally by all the people

condominium (18)—two or more homes or apartments that are joined together but have separate owners

Confucius (46)—a great thinker and writer that lived in ancient China

construction (85)—building

container (121)—a large, box-like metal receptacle used to transport goods on ships and railway cars

contract (64)—make an agreement; e.g., between a village or town and a farming family

cosmetic (85)—a product to beautify the face or skin

courtyard (18)—an open space surrounded by walls or buildings

criteria (146)—standards by which something is judged or categorized

custom (3)—the usual way of doing things

cybercafe (119)—a restaurant or public place where customers pay a small fee to use a computer and the internet

dairy products (128)—products made from milk,

such as cheese, ice cream, yogurt

Daoism (46)—a Chinese religion teaching respect for nature and living in harmony with nature

delta (56)—a flat plain at the mouth of a river

democracy (28)—a political system where people vote for government members and have a say in government decision making

demonstration (28)—a public meeting to express an opinion on an issue

depleted (105)—exhausted, reduced

desert (32)—an area of low rainfall, often less than 200 mm

development (113)—creating changes for a purpose, often involving an increase in industries and services in a place

dialect (78)—a form of a language with different vocabulary and pronunciation

drought (11)—a long period of time without rain

electrical appliances (88)—toasters, mixers, frying pans, coffee pots, and other small machines that run on electricity

elevation (3)—height above sea level

emperors (7)—rulers of China

endangered (81)—threatened with extinction

energy (105)—power, force; e.g., electrical energy

environment (32)—the air, land, and water that we share with all living and non-living things

estimate (50)—form an opinion about how much, how many, etc.

evaluate (31)—to develop an opinion or make a decision based on a set of criteria

export (12)—goods sent to other countries

extended family (92)—a family with three or more generations, usually grandparents, parents, and children

festival (134)—special community celebration

flax (35)—a blue-flowered plant used to make linseed oil and linen cloth

foreign (113)—from outside China

freedoms (28)—the power to make choices for oneself

freight (121)—transportation of goods in containers

fungi (81)—mushrooms, toadstools, molds

generator (125)—a machine that produces electrical energy

ginseng (81)—a plant with a thick, forked root, used in tonics

golden rice bowl (98)—enough money to buy more than the basic needs of food and clothing

graphic organizer (144)—diagrams, tables, or charts used to organize and record information and show relationships

group needs (social needs) (30)—needs that involve people's relationships with others: the need for direction, order, group security, passing on skills and information, work, new ideas and inventions, language, and identity

group wants (social wants) (30)—wants to have a group

need met in a particular way; e.g., to get a certain kind of education, to work at a particular job

Han (12)—the majority ethnic group in China

harmony (46)—an agreeable, balanced state; orderliness

herbal (46)—related to plants or natural sources

humid (52)—a large amount of moisture in the air

hydroelectric (12)—electricity produced by the force of water

import (105)—bring into the country

income (67)—money an individual or family has for spending on basic needs

interdependent (3)—needing each other

interior (123)—inner, away from the coast

internet (91)—a network linking computers around the world

invaders (27)—people who take over by force

iron rice bowl (97)—a Chinese phrase meaning a person is guaranteed a job for life, and so will always eat

irrigation (35)—a constant source of water supplied through ditches or channels

Islam (47)—a religion based on teachings of the prophet Muhammad recorded in the Qur'an

laid off (97)—no longer employing someone

landforms (10)—natural features of the earth, such as plains, hills, and mountains

latitude (30)—the distance north or south of the Equator

leisure time (132)—time not spent at school or work; time to relax or do hobbies

lunar calendar (134)—a 13-month calendar that follows the cycles of the moon

luxury (100)—things wanted that are beyond basic needs

martial arts (133)—skills once used by soldiers to practice self-defense and by monks to improve their concentration

Middle East (39)—roughly includes the area from Libya to Afghanistan

millet (12)—a cereal grain

minority nationalities (12)—ethnic groups with their own language and culture

missionary (47)—a person who brings religious teachings to others

moat (21)—a deep water-filled ditch

Mongolian (32)—associated with the Mongol peoples of Mongolia and Inner Mongolia

mosque (36)—a place of worship for the people who follow Islam

natural resources (12)—raw materials that come from the environment, e.g., wood, water, fish, soil

needs (30)—basic human requirements for survival. People have physical, psychological, and group (social) needs. (*See* basic needs)

news medium (119)—the way news is communicated; plural is "media"

nomadic herders (38)—people who keep herds of sheep and cattle and travel to find new supplies of food for their animals

nuclear family (92)—a husband and wife, or a single parent, and children; a two generation family

nutrients (128)—vitamins and minerals

oasis (38)—a fertile spot in the desert with a water source

One-Child Family Plan (85)—a Chinese government plan to reduce population growth by limiting family size

open policy (24)—a government plan that allowed exchange of goods, ideas, and people between China and other countries

opening to the world (103)—a government plan to allow exchange of goods, ideas, and people between China and other countries

Pacific Rim (2)—all the countries that border on the Pacific Ocean

paddy (52)—a small irrigated rice field

peasant (20)—a rural worker or farmer

pharmacy (53)—a shop dispensing medicines and treatments

Phutonghua (76)—native dialect of Northern China and Beijing

physical needs (30)—needs that must be met to keep the body alive; e.g., food, clothing, shelter, water, physical activity

physical wants (30)—things wanted that are more than enough to keep the body alive, or wants to have a need satisfied in a particular way; e.g., brand-name clothing, luxury foods

pictorial (30)—using pictures

Pinyin (79)—a method of writing Chinese using the Roman alphabet

plateau (10)—a landform with steep sides and fairly level surfaces; often found between mountain ranges

political (28)—providing direction, order, and security to meet group needs

pollution (16)—making unclean or impure, contamination

population (12)—number of people living in a city, area, region, or country

population density (107)—the number of people living in a square kilometer

population growth (105)—the amount the population of a place increases or decreases

porcelain (49)—a thin china made from kaolin clay

port (85)—harbor; where goods are loaded onto and off of ships

precipitation (38)—rain or snow falling to the ground

predict (50)—consider the known facts and suggest what will happen in the future

processed food (131)—food products prepared in factories; not fresh

profit (99)—money made after expenses

psychological needs (30)—needs that affect the mind: comfort, reassurance, love, acceptance, personal security, rules to live by, rest, leisure, challenges, stimulation, achievement

psychological wants (30)—wants to have a psychological need met by a particular person or in a particular way; e.g., to achieve a certain goal or to be loved by a certain person

qigong (133)—a type of healing exercise; a popular martial art for keeping fit and healthy

Qur'an (47)—the holy book of Islam

rent (20)—a portion of the crop given to the landowner as payment for using the land

resident (94)—a person who lives in a building or neighborhood

responsibility (92)—duty

responsibility system (24)—a plan allowing people to work for themselves and make extra money

Roman alphabet (79)—the 26 letters used to write English and many European languages

rudder (49)—the steering mechanism of a boat

rural (23)—in the countryside

scanner (3)—a machine for copying images into a computer

sewage (105)—waste from humans and animals

shrine (90)—a place where religious articles are kept

Silk Road (32)—a caravan route used to carry silk from China to Europe

silt (125)—fine particles of earth carried by a river, dropped to form layers of soil

social needs (*See* **group needs**)

society (46)—all the relationships that exist among the people of a place

sorghum (12)—a tropical cereal grass

space heater (91)—an electrical appliance providing heat to a room; often used in place of a central furnace

Special Economic Zone (112)—area where the Chinese government has encouraged new factories and industries to develop

stir-fry (128)—small pieces of meat and vegetables quickly stirred in a very hot wok

sulfur dioxide (125)—a chemical responsible for acid rain when it mixes with water in the atmosphere

table tennis (133)—ping pong

taijiquan (95)—ancient Chinese exercises often called *tai chi*

technical school (77)—a school where skills for trades such as electrician, welder are taught

technology (3)—the tools and skills of a group of people

telephone village (119)—a village where over 60% of the homes have a private telephone

temple (46)—a religious building or place of worship

terraces (52)—flat steps cut into hillsides used for growing crops

Three Gorges (113)—a narrow river channel on the Chang Jiang flowing through an area of steep cliffs

trade (7)—the exchange of goods between countries

tradition (3)—an idea or way of doing things passed on from older people to younger people for a long time

traditional (7)—done the same way for a long time

transportation (12)—ways of carrying people or goods from one place to another

travel documents (7)—passport, visa

urban (107)—city

values (46)—opinions on what we believe is good or how things ought to be

vendor (14)—a person who sells something

visual (v)—something seen; a photo, illustration, map, or other image

wages (75)—salary

wants (30)—things you desire or that you think can be used to satisfy a need. People have physical, psychological, and group (social) wants. Wants are learned.

Western (93)—refers to anything that is non-Chinese or non-Asian

Western medicine (80)—mainly uses surgery, manufactured drugs, and specialized medical equipment to treat illnesses

wok (97)—a Chinese cooking pot

work unit (18)—a Chinese term referring to the place where people work

wushu (133)—also known as *kung fu*; a popular martial art form

yak (41)—a long-haired ox of Tibet

yurt (32)—a round tent made from animal hides

Pronunciation List

Beijing	(bay jing)	capital of China
Chengdu	(cheng doo)	city in South China
Chang Jiang	(chang jyang)	Yangtze River
Hohot	(hohu hot)	city in Mongolian Grasslands
Hong Kong	(siang gang)	city in South China
Lhasa	(lar sa)	city on Tibetan Plateau
nihao	(nee how)	hello; how are you?
qigong	(chee gong)	type of healing exercise
Shanghai	(shang high)	city in South China
Shenzhen	(shun zen)	city in South China
taijiquan	(tie chee chuan)	type of martial art
Turpan	(toor phan)	city in Northwest Desert
Urumqi	(oo room chee)	city in Northwest Desert
Xiao Kang	(see au kung)	name of a village
wushu	(woo shoo)	type of martial art
xie xie	(shie shie)	thank you
jizhe	(gee dzer)	reporter

INDEX

Key
▲ chart ● map ■ photo/illustration

Key
▲ chart ● map ■ photo/illustration

Key

▲ chart   ● map   ■ photo/illustration

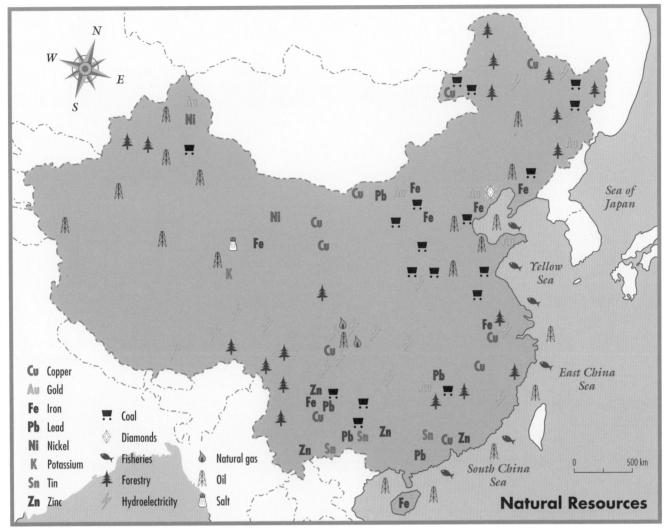

Natural Resources

Cu Copper
Au Gold
Fe Iron
Pb Lead
Ni Nickel
K Potassium
Sn Tin
Zn Zinc

🛒 Coal
◇ Diamonds
🐟 Fisheries
🌲 Forestry
⚡ Hydroelectricity
💧 Natural gas
🗼 Oil
🧂 Salt

Sea of Japan
Yellow Sea
East China Sea
South China Sea

0   500 km

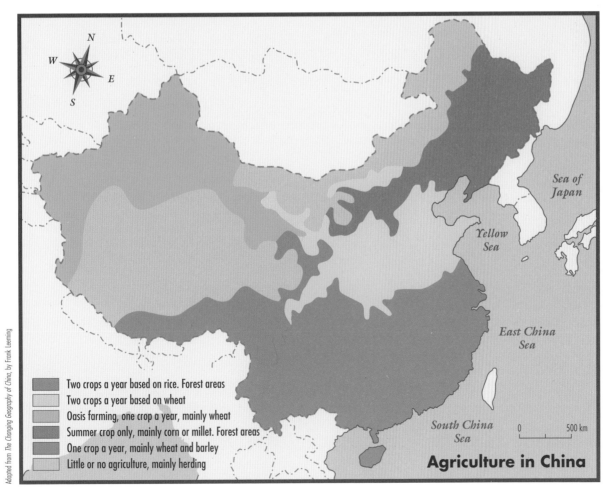

Agriculture in China

Two crops a year based on rice. Forest areas
Two crops a year based on wheat
Oasis farming, one crop a year, mainly wheat
Summer crop only, mainly corn or millet. Forest areas
One crop a year, mainly wheat and barley
Little or no agriculture, mainly herding

Sea of Japan
Yellow Sea
East China Sea
South China Sea

0   500 km

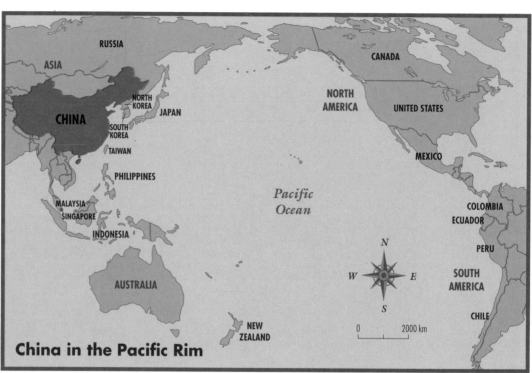

China in the Pacific Rim

RUSSIA
ASIA
CHINA
NORTH KOREA
JAPAN
SOUTH KOREA
TAIWAN
PHILIPPINES
MALAYSIA
SINGAPORE
INDONESIA
AUSTRALIA
NEW ZEALAND

CANADA
NORTH AMERICA
UNITED STATES
MEXICO
Pacific Ocean
COLOMBIA
ECUADOR
PERU
SOUTH AMERICA
CHILE

0   2000 km

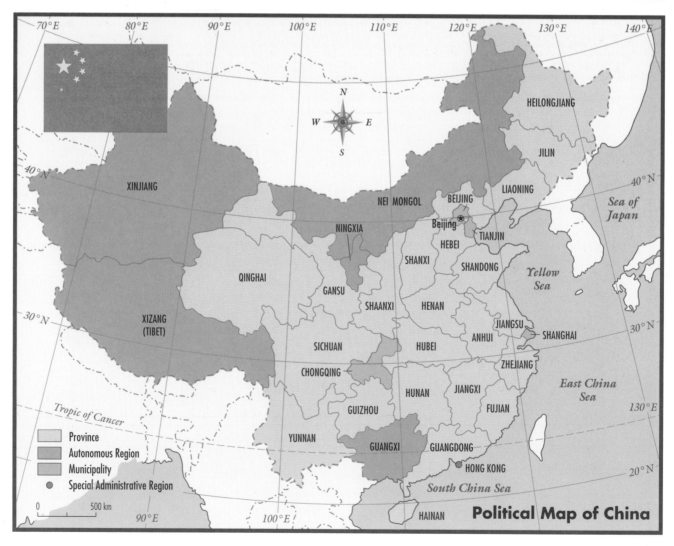

Political Map of China

HEILONGJIANG
JILIN
LIAONING
XINJIANG
NEI MONGOL
BEIJING
Beijing
TIANJIN
NINGXIA
HEBEI
SHANXI
SHANDONG
QINGHAI
GANSU
SHAANXI
HENAN
XIZANG (TIBET)
SICHUAN
HUBEI
ANHUI
SHANGHAI
CHONGQING
ZHEJIANG
HUNAN
JIANGXI
FUJIAN
GUIZHOU
YUNNAN
GUANGXI
GUANGDONG
HONG KONG
HAINAN

Sea of Japan
Yellow Sea
JIANGSU
East China Sea
South China Sea

Tropic of Cancer

Province
Autonomous Region
Municipality
● Special Administrative Region

0   500 km